The ⟨ Almanac for 2021

by

Kevin Ahern

DavinciPress Publishers
Corvallis, Oregon

First Edition

The Odd Farmer's Almanac for 2021

Copyright © 2020 DavinciPress & Kevin Ahern

Introduction

Welcome to *The Odd Farmer's Almanac for 2021*. I have wanted to write an almanac for a long time and I enjoy creating puns and verses. I also strive to be different, and my favorite thing to do is to make people laugh. Put all of those together and you get *The Odd Farmer's Almanac*. If you've bought my limerick and related books previously (URL below), you know how much I love rhymes and puns.

Hopefully, you're starting off the new year on the right foot and this year will be better than last year's train wreck. What looms in this new year? Well, unlike other almanacs, I'm not going to try to predict anything. No weather predictions, no visions of the future, and no astrology. The only future things you'll see here are well-established astronomical phenomena, and they're fairly brief.

You're going to see a LOT of silliness here. The world needs more silliness. Unless it is quoted text from someone else, I wrote everything you see here. I hope you enjoy my book as much as I enjoyed putting it together. I love to hear from fans. You can reach me at limericks@davincipress.com

I'm also on Facebook (kevin.g.ahern), Twitter (@ahernk1), and the Web (www.davincipress.com).

If you go to my Web address above, you can access all of the info about buying my books. Many of my books are actually FREE downloads, so check it out.

Kevin

The Odd Farmer's Almanac for 2021

JANUARY 2021

It would be easy to dismiss January as the "hangover month." It certainly starts out that way, but hangovers don't typically last all month and January always does, so there must be a better description. Things that last all of January include holiday bills, football, coldness, and the desire to be in any other month.

Unlike months which either have something notable about them or that lead to other months that do, January doesn't do much but deliver us to February and, as you'll see next month, that's the weirdest one of the year.

> *Ever wonder where "right foot" came to be used as it does? Well, at least as far back as Shakespeare, starting something badly meant using the "wrong foot." This was partly rooted in superstition. We know that every journey starts with a single step. If you start your journey with the "wrong foot," how well do you expect the journey to go?*

January is named for the Roman god Janus, who was the gatekeeper. The month had a troubled childhood, not even existing in the earliest Roman calendars, and it came into being only to help keep the rest of the calendar in line with the actual astronomical events giving us seasons. January is the time of resolution making and breaking and is welcomed gleefully by owners of gyms, diet products, running clothes manufacturers, and is rued by alcohol producers, dessert makers, and cigarette distributors. By the end of the month, those groups switch places thanks to the fact that resolution breaking is one of the great American pastimes. Makers of products like Spandex think January is super, since it seems to win with both groups of people.

More vacations get planned in January than in any other month, since thinking about anything but January is good for mental health in the middle of winter. The days successively get longer as the month moves further along, but that only serves to make it *seem* longer. That January is the longest month of the year and February is the shortest one is a sadistic joke of early calendar makers. Why not average out January with February?

> May and March, July and Oct, August and December
> These longest months have 31, try hard to remember
> 30 days for Jan and June and April, Sept, November
> Leaving 29 for Feb to keep or 30 in a year of leap

We could give one of January's days to February and everyone would be happy. Think about it. If you moved Martin Luther King day to February, you'd have a holiday to break up February and you'd lose a day in January to boot. 30 and 29 days for the first two months makes sense and on leap years, you'd have 30 and 30.

Finally, speaking of things over our heads, here is astronomy info for January - New Moon - January 13; half-moons on the 6th and 20th and full on the 28th If you're into meteor showers, the Quadrantids are January 2-3. On January 11, Jupiter and Mercury will appear close in the sky, but may be hard to view. On the same day, Venus and the moon will appear close. The moon and Mars will appear close on January 20 and Mercury will be at a high point in the sky on the 26th.

The Odd Farmer's Almanac for 2021

Some furnaces get coaled in the winter

January First
1959
This is a Cuban holiday
The joy felt here was brief
When Castro said that he would stay
And Batista said he'd leave

Raining cats and dogs isn't as bad as hailing taxis

January Second
1974
As the oil boycott
Saps U.S. power
Speed limit cut to
55 miles per hour

January Third
1521
Martin Luther was a man
Who didn't know his station
And so in fifteen twenty one
Got ex-communication

It wasn't all that bad, you know
As it seemed at first glance
Because his followers would go
Become the Protest-ants

January Fourth
1974
In nineteen hundred seven four
Dick Nixon's planned escape
Involved attempts to shut a door
By holding onto tapes

It didn't work, he lost the case
And caused a lot of crap
Most telling thing he had to face?
That eighteen minute gap

January Fifth
1998
Sonny Bono died this day
Some say it wasn't fair
His music got a lot of play
He had a lot to Cher

January Sixth
1838
An internet was made today
By someone named Sam Morse
Its dots and dashes led the way
But downloads were the worst

I didn't save money for a trip to Mexico, so now I Can'tcun

January Seventh
1789
George Washington, as we all know
Led army insurrection
He didn't have too far to go
To win this first election

January Eighth
1946
A "Hound Dog" artist gets a vote
For being quite the star
On this day Elvis we should note
Received his first guitar

He sang like no one ever did
As seen in TV clips
The networks censored him a bit
No shots below the hips

Hippies were hairy pot-ters

> "If you try to fail, and succeed, which have you done?"
> – George Carlin

"Mr. Ed" debuted 1/5/1961

The Earth is closest to the sun on January 2

"Mr. Bean" - Rowan Atkinson born 1/6/1955

The Odd Farmer's Almanac for 2021

January Ninth
1776
The patriot named Thomas Paine
Did not sit on the fence
Today we could use his advice
He published "Common Sense"

January Tenth
1861
William Seward on this date
Had reason to be jolly
For he began as Sec. of State
But got called out for folly

As Lincoln's man he did great things
And led expansive surges
Today I hear that Russia stings
From his Alaska purchase

January Eleventh
1909
Hooray for Teddy Roosevelt
Good news Grand Canyon sent
His declaration widely felt
A national monument

1973
The baseball rules got changed once more
It made the N.L. bitter
When A.L. swapped their pitchers for
A designated hitter

January Twelfth
1932
Ophelia Wyatt Caraway
Who came from Arkansas
Was voted senator on this day
A female first in law

> The Spanish word for cat
> ought to be 'purrito'

> "If you find it hard to laugh at
> yourself, I would be happy
> to do it for you."
> – Groucho Marx

"A fool and his money are soon elected" - Will Rogers

January Thirteenth
1929
Out Tombstone, Arizona way
Historians all shall
Make note that Wyatt Earp this day
Met his O.K. corral

> "The Mummy" is
> the stiff of legends

January Fourteenth
1954
The wedding bells were ringing then
For Marilyn Monroe
Did she think she would strike out when
She wed Dimaggio?

> In parachute school, you drop
> out when you graduate

January Fifteenth
1967
The Packers met the Chiefs today
In California stupor
Two football leagues came out to play
The first bowl that was Super

January Sixteenth
1919
This day for drinkers is the worst
And doesn't get respect
It made it hard to slake one's thirst
Prohibition took effect

January Seventeenth
1966
A brand new TV music show
The network? NBC's
No zoo would any of them know
Hey, hey, it's The Monkees

> "Halo" is angel for "hi"

Some clergy are parsonal trainers

The Odd Farmer's Almanac for 2021

January Eighteenth
1882
A.A. Milne, born on this day
Wrote many books, it's true
Gave animals a lot to say
And one of them was Pooh

1958
The Boston Bruins led the way
It was a great occasion
When Willie O'Ree got to play
NHL integration

> A car bomber blew the coupe

January Nineteenth
1809
Ravens, hearts, and pendulae
Are eerie things we know
Because of one born on this day
Edgar Allen Poe

2007
In China now, we see what sells
Is capitalism king?
Today on Chinese soil dwells
McDonalds in Beijing

> Deer breeders don't get rich, but they make a few bucks

January Twentieth
1961
"Ask not what your country can do for you"
He said on this occasion
The man was JFK, it's true
At his inauguration

January Twenty First
1976
In London and in Paris there
Was really quite a sight
Simultaneously in the air
The first two Concorde flights

January Twenty Second
1951
Fidel Castro, on the mound
Couldn't be much madder
He got kicked out from a game
Because he hit a batter

January Twenty Third
1957
The Wham-O business got a boost
On this day it is known
Because these folks today produced
The first Frisbee ever thrown

January Twenty Fourth
1935
Opinions vary wildly for
The tastes found in an ale
Today the picture clouded more
When canned beer went on sale

January Twenty Fifth
1961
Upon this day we note success
Of President Kennedy
The 1st to face the White House press
In front of live TV

January Twenty Sixth
1950
The Delhi population was
Amazed with what 'twas seeing
The Indian Republic was the cause
By coming into being

> When I went to a metric urologist, I centipeed into a cup

Rowan and Martin's Laugh-In Debuted 1/22/68

John Belushi born 1/24/49

The worst part of the job for carpet installers is tacks time

> "I wish I were dumber so I could be more certain about my opinions. It looks fun."
> – Scott Adams

The Odd Farmer's Almanac for 2021

January Twenty Seventh
1970
John Lennon had a lot to say
A musician and a charmer
He recorded in this single day
His classic, "Instant Karma"

> The Queen of the Nile liked to show some leg, but Nefertiti

January Twenty Eighth
1985
A lot of dedicated work
Began to be unfurled
Recording artists this day made
The song "We Are the World"

January Twenty Ninth
1936
This is a baseball date that fans
Should certainly remember
Cuz the Hall of Fame unveiled its plans
Inducting the first members

January Thirtieth
1956
Elvis Presley
Making news
Today recorded
"Blue Suede Shoes"

January Thirty First
1990
Of capitalism, Khrushchev said
"Communism will crush ya"
But on this day McDonalds fed
Its first folks back in Russia

> The period leading up to Britain ruling the seas was the Phase that Launched a Thousand Ships

---

> "At every party there are two kinds of people – those who want to go home and those who don't. The trouble is, they are usually married to each other."
> – Ann Landers

> Birds in Valdez, AK wake up oily in the morning

A Royal Pain in the Neck

An actress known as Meghan Markle
Has a smile with lots of sparkle
On one fine day she met a guy
The second son of Princess Di

Who told her that his name was Harry
And the two decided they would marry

But that is not the end of story
Wedding a Prince so charming
She's entered into territory
That might be quite alarming

For her in life, there's so much more
Than just a royal wedding
Recall his family's noted for
A bit of wife beheading

A texting driver is a carred reader

> A candle fell in love with Sir Lancelot, but he preferred darkness, so she went out for the knight

The Odd Farmer's Almanac for 2021

An Ode to January

Corvallis winter's one month in
No arctic blasts, it's scary
So odd to have such mildness at
The end of January

But no complaints, don't get me wrong
It's good last year concluded
More absence at the gym each day
Not what was resoluded

But that's OK, instead go forth
And pour yourself a beer
To mark the anniversary cuz
It happens every year

Then as you celebrate, rejoice
This one fact that's worth knowing
It still is two months more until
The grass begins re-growing

The Pillsbury Doughboy doesn't date anymore. He's been burned too many times

In September 2007, Kevin Shelley broke 46 wooden toilet seats with his head in one minute - a world record

---

January

The January darkness always
Tries our endurance. Can we last?
The days are slowly getting longer
Optimism getting stronger
Let the season have its bender
We'll rejoice in winter's splendor
And when it's snowing day and night
We'll all admire the piles of white

End of the Season

New year's Day is here oh golly
Time for resolutions
So pack up all the trees and holly
Christmas's conclusion

Resolutions I like to extol
They're part of a brand new year's goal
I told my friend Will
That I'm on the pill
Cuz I'm practicing girth control

In This New Year

Fight darkness with light
Wrongness with right
No matter the consequence
Fight

Make ignorant smart
Change ugly to art
Whatever the reason
Start

Turn timid to strong
Noises to song
Participate and
Belong

Give riches to poor
Culture to boors
Help everybody
Soar

Set broken to mend
Let mixtures blend
My thinking has now reached the
End

January Gloom

January brings winter chills
And all those unpaid Christmas bills
Some people hoping for solutions
Atone by making resolutions

To trim and build up their physiques
They exercise a couple weeks
And then complain and whine and crab
That they have still got all their flab

There's little here to celebrate
I think it's best to sit and wait
For spring

As the photon took off for his flight
He packed up his things really tight
When asked why he dragged
Just one Duffel bag
He said he was traveling light

Frosty Snowman's favorite song
Leaves him all feeling mellow
So little children, sing along
"Freeze a Jolly Good Fellow"

My girlfriend of late has been miffed
Because of my lame birthday gift
Now how would I know
She didn't like snow?
It's too bad, if you get my drift

The Odd Farmer's Almanac for 2021

Tropic Topic
When Cuba's first
To space is shot
Havana will have
A Castronaut

Income Tics
Here's hoping there are
Major cashes
For making rhymes
Like Ogden Nash's

Feline Line
The cat said from
The shelter space
"Please get meowt"
"Of this place"

Getting Heavy
If you have trouble
With your weight
Try to lighten
Up your plate

Wash Out
Though I clearly
Stated my wishes
No one ever
Did the dishes

Think Stink
Skunk breeders all
Are most absurd
Each one a person
Of phew words

No Match
As for old films
Someone has tossed
He who acetates
Is lost

SeXY
The teenage girl
Is overjoyed
When the guy called back
Her spirits boyed

High Seize
Blackbeard's slogan
Gotta admire it
Proclaims that God
Is his co-pirate

Wiped Out
The chimney sweep
Knew what to do
Called in to work
Sick with the flue

Internet Carrier
Moses speaking
To the crowd
Downloaded tablets
From the cloud

Two For One
Here's a question
No one wants
Do two nuances
Make a duance?

By Nary
The computer chip
Who has a cough
Just made mistakes
A wee bit off

Wonder Brad
The bakery show
On the telly
Starred Bread Pitt
And Angelina Jelly

Birth Daze
The obstetrician
There I swear
Works for ladies
Ready to bear

<u>Short Cut</u>
A local lass
With golden hair
With her fencing coach
Had a sworded affair

When human cannonballs get fired, they have a job

January is National Bath Safety Month

Samuel Morse dashed off many letters

January is Thyroid Awareness Month

In LA, beachgoers do SoCal distancing

Page 11

The Odd Farmer's Almanac for 2021

Career Considerations

I thought I'd cruise selling shoes
But there was a dispute
Resulting in a problem so
The boss gave me the boot

I liked my railroad work a lot
But sadly, I got sacked
They said the reason was because
I always got sidetracked

A sanitation engineering job
Gave hope to me - I jumped
But on day two the boss declared
That I had just been dumped

The credit union hired me next
And offered many perks
But it was bad, so now I'm sad
Lost interest in my work

I loved to help build houses
'Twas work that I adored
But after doing it a while
I quit cuz I was board

I wrote a script to be performed
They say it was absurd
Each line was funny with a pun
A silly play on words

Then Binyons hired me quickly to
Put products on the shelf
But then I fell in their machine
Made a spectacle of myself

I moved into accountancy
But rapidly got tossed
I stumbled all around a lot
With no balance, I was lost

Career Considerations

I worked in glue, but now I'm blue
There's no way to wordsmith it
The problem was, I think because
I just could not stick with it

I joined the crew at Starbucks but
Quite quickly I resigned
I liked the people, but quickly got
Tired of the daily grind

Selling computer parts was next
Really thought I'd thrive
But I got fired one day because
I totally lost my drive

Then working as a butler seemed
So very grand to me
But quickly I found out that it
Was not my cup of tea

The orange juice factory had a job
At first it looked quite great
But I got fired because they said
I couldn't concentrate

A job in gardening seemed to work
Although I was a fool
Important things I didn't know
Included the ground rules

So next I went and made a blanket
Then found a store that sold it
Alas they didn't do too well
And very quickly folded

So now I do not have a job
I sit around and wonder
Do meteorologists feel like me
That someone stole their thunder?

The hot dog complaint came from an Oscar Mayer whiner

The Odd Farmer's Almanac for 2021

Signs of the Times

This verse about professions lists
The signs where people work
They are not what they seem at all
Each one has got a quirk

A podiatrist knows that things go wrong
With the way that your feet feel
His sign proclaims "You'll Come To Me
Because Time Wounds All Heels"

A shoe repairer down the street
Thinks fondly of his role
His sign says "I Shall Heel You"
"And Maybe Save Your Sole"

The gynecologist every day
Most surely earns her dime
Her sign says "I Am Always At"
"Your Cervix All The Time"

The optometrist's much longer sign
Cuts quickly to the chase
"Don't See What You Are Looking For?"
"Then You're At The Right Place"

Some plumber wisdom echoes through
This very useful tip
Declaring that "You Shouldn't Be"
"Asleeping with that drip"

I get embarrassed reading what
My electrician's sign exhorts
To customers it dares to say
"Let Us Remove Your Shorts"

The obstetrician's office door
Beside the holly bush
Has a sign that says quite simply
That you should "Push, Push, Push"

Paying with a credit card is a buy pass operation

Signs of the Times

Our veterinarian has a sign
For when she is away
It has the jive "I'm Back In Five"
"But Meanwhile SIT! & STAY!"

The electric company's office sign
Is very often cited
It says "If You Don't Pay Your Bill"
"We Know You'll Be Delighted"

The dealer of some fine used cars
Whose lot is down the street
Says "If You Miss One Payment"
"You'll Be Back On Your Feet"

The muffler shop has one big sign
It really is quite stunning
"No Need For You To Phone Ahead"
"Cuz We Can Hear You Coming"

The radiator guy has got
A sign that is unique
It says his shop's "The Best place
You'll Ever Take a Leak"

And last, the propane station's sign
Is trying to spread goodwill
It simply says to everyone
"Thank Heaven For Little Grills"

"Good advice is something a man gives when he is too old to set a bad example."
– Francois de La Rochefoucauld

"A computer once beat me at chess, but it was no match for me at kick boxing."
– Emo Philips

The Odd Farmer's Almanac for 2021

FEBRUARY 2021

Congratulations! You made it through January, a month some consider the cruelest one. You may not agree, but January unquestionably is the coolest one, at least in the northern hemisphere. So, we exit the month that left us with hangovers of a year we'd just as soon forget and plunge into . . . the weirdest month.

In February, we get 1) President's Day - a holiday that isn't a holiday unless you're a federal employee and is the time retailers have decreed is when houseware sales should occur (?); 2) Groundhog's Day - a holiday that is a non-holiday unless you live in Punxsutawney, PA, where an innocent groundhog gets drug out of its warm and peaceful burrow once a year to get its picture taken by dozens of photographers while being held by a man in a silly hat; and 3) St. Valentine's Day, a holiday with religious roots and dedicated to courtly love that absolutely no one gets off. The man for whom the holiday is named was a 3rd century Roman who happens to be the patron saint of . . . . . (wait for it) . . . . (you'll never guess) . . . . EPILEPSY (look it up). So how did February 14 become sweethearts' day? You don't want to know. At least February is the shortest month, but even that is weird: 28 days in three years out of every four when it has 29, except only in century years evenly divisible by four when . . . oh never mind.

> The word 'hangover' was not originally associated with drinking too much alcohol, though the phenomenon of a hangover has been described for over 3000 years. Originally the word 'hangover' was used to describe unfinished business. Only around the turn of the 20th century did it acquire its current meaning.

February is the purgatory of months - too far away from the start of spring (no matter what the groundhog says) and struggling to escape the last clutches of winter. In many U.S. locales, February is the time of greatest snowfall, since warmer air holds more moisture and . . . this is turning into a meteorology lesson. Instead, it's time for our monthly look upwards. In February, we get half moons on the 4th and the 19th. The new moon pops up on February 11 and it becomes full on the 27th. The moon and Mars appear close in the sky on the 18th and Mercury is high in the morning sky on the 24th.

> On Valentines day, my friend quips
> Listen carefully - follow these tips
> To get lots of kisses
> This one never misses
> Remember - you just need tulips

You may know February is Black History Month, but were you aware it is also Canned Food Month, Dog Training Education Month, National Bird Feeding Month, National Cat Health Month, National Grapefruit Month and Pet Dental Health Month? Well, now you know. Celebrate gently - remember New Year's Eve?

The Odd Farmer's Almanac for 2021

February First
1896
Puccini had a lot of sway
On opera it appeared
One final product came this day
When La Boheme premiered

> **Viagra is marketed to hillbillies as "Mount an' Do"**

February Second
1996
Gene Kelly brought a lot of joy
With steps that had much grace
Today they brought this dancing boy
To the pearly gates

February Third
1959
When Buddy Holly took a ride
It later was revealed
To be the day the music died
In an Iowa corn field

February Fourth
1941
To keep morale up for our troops
When loved ones they depart
The entertaining USO
On this day got its start

> **People who arrange those dried flower things are old growth florists**

February Fifth
1922
Publishing takes lots of ink
Across all categories
So Readers Digest on this day
Began abridging stories

February Sixth
1977
Queen Elizabeth on this day
Was surely filled with glee
Because 'twas now she celebrated
Her silver jubilee

February Seventh
1964
If you were at JFK airport
You'd never see anything zani-ah
Upon this day four lads did land
And kicked off Beatle mania

February Eighth
1983
Wayne Gretzky's hockey skills
Were certainly myriad
Today he set a record with
Four goals in just one period

February Ninth
1994
A great day for South Africa
After what he underwent
We're speaking of Mandela
Who became their President

February Tenth
1763
The Treaty of Paris, signed today
Received a mighty roar
From people who celebrated the end
Of the French and Indian war

February Eleventh
1953
A boy who could fly and never grow old
Some people considered it weird
Well, strange or not, this very day
Peter Pan premiered

> **I tried one of those mail-order bride services and now I can't wait for my Czech in the mail**

Sidebars:
- John Wayne's real name was Marion Morrison
- Electric German cars are Volts Wagons
- "Blazing Saddles" released 2/7/1974
- Ham soup is an add hock meal

The Odd Farmer's Almanac for 2021

> **The mocking humor of a clever knight is known as sircasm**

February Twelfth
1809
Abraham Lincoln, born today
Made slavery illegal
And Charles Darwin also born today
Got fame with HMS Beagle

February Thirteenth
1866
Jesse James, the criminal
Along with brother Frank
Made history this day because
He robbed his very first bank

February Fourteenth
1876
Elisha Gray and Alex Bell
Wish they could have called home
With the news that on this day they both
Applied to patent telephones

"Groundhog Day" released 2/12/93

> **My father's brother who drinks too much is my druncle**

February Fifteenth
399 BC
Socrates got
The awful truth
Sentenced for corrupting
The minds of youth

February Sixteenth
1937
A patent issued on this day
Gave fabric to build a style on
DuPont was the inventor
And gave it the name of Nylon

February Seventeenth
1938
Color TV was born this day
'Twas quite the occasion
I think it was too early, though
For them to change the station

February Eighteenth
1885
Mark Twain was happy on this day
It meant a lot to him
The publication of his book
"The Adventures of Huckleberry Finn"

February Nineteenth
1473
Copernicus was born this day
He got under the church's skin
For saying the Earth did orbit the sun
To his mother, it revolved around him

February Twentieth
1962
John Glenn was blasted into space
Inside a Mercury probe
Becoming the first American
To orbit 'round the globe

Self-help book for trees – "I'm Oak, You're Oak"

> **Fake African news is propuganda**

February Twenty First
1878
The world of telemarketing
On this day was increased
When 50 names were printed in
The first phone book released

February Twenty Second
1879
Frank Woolworth sold his merchandise
For five cents, never more
In Utica, New York this day
Inside his very first store

> My father's brother who drinks too much is my druncle

February Twenty Third
1960
Another day for Woolworth's
A civil rights uproar
White students joined with black ones
At a Winston-Salem store

February Twenty Fourth
1991
General Schwarzkopf, on this day
Exactly knew the score
Directing all the ground troops
Beginning the Gulf war

February Twenty Fifth
1913
Today's not a day for people who
Hate government on their backs
The sixteenth amendment got approved
Authorizing the income tax

February Twenty Sixth
1933
In San Francisco
On this date
Ground was broken
For the Golden Gate

February Twenty Seventh
1908
Hard to believe it wasn't til
Nineteen hundred eight
That Oklahoma territory
Became the 46th state

February Twenty Eighth
1827
What a celebration
The biggest New Orleans saw
Its birth we recognize today
The first big Mardi Gras

Double Meanings

To **burglarize** is stealing things
We know that it is true
They also are the things through which
The thief is seeing you

I really am **avoidable**
When I have morning breath
It's also what bull fighters do
When they're dodging death

Eyedroppers put the medicine
In eyes, yes they assist
And also help describe the work
Of bad ophthalmologists

In prison, there is much **control**
Of everybody's fate
It's also one way we describe
An unruly inmate

The **counterfeiters** copy dough
In million dollar sets
And also work in kitchens where
They shape the cabinets

A **purchase** is the way we get
The goods to pack in cases
And how we pay for every bet
That goes at Greyhound races

Barium is an element
Of which the Earth is full
And also what we do at every
Chemist's funeral

Eclipse describes the darkness that
A moon transit is giving
And what an English barber does
To earn a decent living

> Motor home owners get away from it all by taking it with them

> Bubble Wrap® was invented as a type of wallpaper

> The transparent billboard about cancer is a clear sign of trouble

The Odd Farmer's Almanac for 2021

Oregon Winter

It's winter here in Oregon
With all of us resisting
Depression from the fact we've had
Two months of non-stop misting

We never get a blizzard here
Though it is often foggy
And forty days of rain can make
The walking rather soggy

Another benefit we get
Is quite the equalizer
We never need to put upon
Our skin a moisturizer

So go ahead and mock us now
You will not hurt our feelings
Cuz we're too busy cleaning off
The mold from bathroom ceilings

Midwinter Muse

How bright the sun
Is shining now
Winter's backing off
And how!

We're ready
Please come join us, Spring
And fill up every
Living thing

Above the Clouds

What's out beyond the clouds we see?
Way up so far above?
Does outer space have heaven's grace
With ancestors that we love?

Or could it be unhappily
A fact we have to face
That what's out there devoid of air
Is only empty space?

February Finale

The February days are few
Think groundhogs and valentines
With Mardi Gras between the two
And Presidents' Day signs

We're ready for the winter's end
And picture it Hawaiian
But reality we can't suspend
It's like wet dandelions

Perhaps that is too bleak and grim
The days are not so stark
And daffodils are looking prim
As light gains on the dark

The arctic air's no longer near
So spring is now a dream
The surest sign of it is here
Spring training for baseball teams

Barbers are shearholders

Shout Em Up
The old west lawman
Chasing a perp
Didn't say much
Quiet Earp

Good Marx in School
The Russian student's
Very glad
His diploma makes him
A Lenin grad

Overdrawn
That guy from Prague
Is dense as heck
I'd say that he's
One blank Czech

Before Computers

There was a time not long ago
In the pre-computer phase
That memory was something
You lost in your sunset days

Applications were for getting jobs
Programs were on TV
A cursor was a potty mouth
And at banks you got CDs

A keyboard was like a piano
A virus was a cold or the flu
A hard drive was going to grandma's house
A web's what a spider looked through

A mouse was not desirable
A mouse pad was its home
And if your floppy was 3.5 inches
It was something to bemoan

Naught Counting

I read the other afternoon
About the things there are
Ten to the one hundred particles
A number most bizarre

That's when I heard a tiny voice
Express a tiny thought
"Oh yes, but have you ever tried"
"To count things that are not?"

I cocked my head in wonder
How many could there be?
If they are not, they really
Haven't got a quantity

But no way I'll be stymied
I'll total them for you
I just need special numbers
Imaginary ones will do

My computer has the Spamish flu

Charmin is hind sanitizer

Ibuprofanity - what you say when your Advil doesn't work

"Patriotism is your conviction that this country is superior to all others because you were born in it."
– George Bernard Shaw

I'm having a do
Don't get too excited
It's a quarantine party
And no one's invited

"If you live to be one hundred, you've got it made. Very few people die past that age."
– George Burns

Sometimes I sit and wonder why
With no clue whatsoever
Like why do hair cells have to die
But fat cells live forever?

Asthma:
The wheezin' for the season

The Odd Farmer's Almanac for 2021

Shorties

Norway, Man
That Oslo guy
Sure did complain
His ankle svelte up
From a sprain

Stoned
A marbleous statue
Please don't pan it
They're very often
Taken for granite

Stuck With the Bill
A Chinese restaurant
I like oodles
Does acupuncture
With pins and noodles

Mess Hall
My coffee table
Looks like an ocean
From a drink I spilled
In one fluid motion

Swamped
That southerner's not
Easily persuaded
But his swamp has been
Bayou degraded

Dressing Up
That Caesar salad's bad
But do not grab it
Instead, I'll take
A stab at it

Slice of Life
The Dominoes guy
Just yelled out 'what?"
When his life in two
Pizzas was cut

Taking Five
Consider the wisdom
Of pastor Hal
For church donations
He's got PrayPal

The pitcher came from a pour family

The sneaky virus Covid its tracks

Some people spend a fortune so they can circle the world. I drink some beer and the world circles around me - Anonymous

---

Shorties

Happy Notes
Your grocery bags
That have iPhones
Are what I'd call
Sacks o' phones

Hot Ride
Starbucks was not
In the wild west so
A couple of guys
Made Pony Espresso

Paperback Rider
A bookworm here
Could not resist
Putting "Waiting for Godot"
On her Beckett list

Unihorn
The neutered horse
With just one horn
I love its name
A eunuch-corn

Point Well Taken
She's got support
I must concur
Her middle finger
Sticks up for her

Dead Heads
The funeral parlor's
Coffee astounds
Perhaps they're using
Burial grounds?

Wheezer Geezer
Grandfather now
Is at that stage
Where he has reached
A gripe old age

Flying Solo
Princess Leia
In outer spaces
Looked for love
In Alderaan places

The Odd Farmer's Almanac for 2021

Shorties

Stop Short
When a storyteller
Makes you wail
It's time to go
Cut off his tale

Heck of a Deal
Panama's canal
Is truly great
A very massive
Inside strait

No Crater Good
A Chinese astronaut
Very soon
Will take a wok up
On the moon

Hello Dali
Painter Dali
Ate flakes with zeal
Because he really
Liked surreal

Stop On It
Please don't exercise
Your throttle
Any time
You use the bottle

Nut Quacker
Donald Duck
Was up and gone
Arising at the
Quack of dawn

Mum's the Word
A group attack by
Evil mimes
Resulted in
Unspeakable crimes

Fishy Character
Deep sea divers
Seeking treasure
Function well
Under pressure

Shorties

Duly Wedded
The Dating Game couple
Does not disparage
The idea behind
Game marriage

Short Stops
Little Leaguers
At the platter
Each of them
A peanut batter

Old Goaled
When I retire
You gotta believe
I'll be taking
Maturity leave

Hoe, Hoe, Hoe
The Jolly Green Giant's
Wanting more
Assistance from
His peas corps

I Kid You Not
The octomom
And octodad
Say they're both
Stork raving mad

Sandy Way Go
Walking the Desert
Seems to me
To be unreal
Long time, no sea

About a Stout
A drink of beer
At home at night
Helps me to wet
My appetite

Cooking Oils
When the gallery caught
On fire I learned
They had a bad case
Of art burn

Electric German cars are Volts Wagons

Fishing gives me a haddock

The "Plant Lady" is a hoarder culturist

Page 21

Oxymorons

Oxymorons everywhere
They really are absurd
Described in verses here below
In each one's bolded words

I don't think I'm the first to notice
And will not be the last
But how can something that occurred
Be in the **recent past**?

Now if you ask him nicely
He'll kill you with a roar
I guess that is what happens when
There is a **civil war**

Can I touch it or is it fake?
It's such insanity
To have a concept we describe
As **virtual reality**

The dinosaurs are gone because
Of asteroidal strife
Let's let them rest in peace and not
Declare them **extinct life**

The appraiser who was looking there
At my old antique set
Just gave to me what he described
As an **exact estimate**

Then what about the people
Who sneer at someone smugly?
And then declare to all nearby
That they are **pretty ugly**

I thought I got the only one
When I bought my antique
But there must be another one
If it is **most unique**

You never know of other folks
So follow this advice
It isn't clear what to expect
When someone's **awful nice**

Canadians have Type Eh personalities

Oxymorons

Another murky phrase out there
Ought never to be used
Because the person using it
Is **clearly** quite **confused**

And tell me please if you think I
Am being too erratic
When I declare out loud that I
Am rather **mildly ecstatic**

Unless it is electricity
It makes no sense to me
How anyone could talk about
The **current history**

Museums also get to me
They really make me groan
When something there is on display
Thanks to a **permanent loan**

And of museums, I declare
I'm at the end of my wits
How is it possible they could have
A bunch of **private exhibits**?

So when it comes to oxymorons
I think all these are shoo-ins
The museum has the best of all
Their collection of **restored ruins**

Mohammed Ali

"Float like a butterfly"
"Sting like a bee"
Those were the words
Of Mohammed Ali

He was the greatest of all time
And knew the power of using rhyme
It's sad, but true, each one agrees
Boxing gave him Parkinson's Disease

The Origami Society sees its membership in creasing

The Odd Farmer's Almanac for 2021

MARCH 2021

"In like a lion, out like a lamb," or so some would have you think. March is a transition month, and so, is prone to extremes. It's a pretty good month, though, as months go, unless you happened to be Julius Caesar. Turns out he wasn't the only one who had to beware of the Ides of March, as that date was also the time that Romans were supposed to settle their debts. In the U.S., we have the same feeling about the Ides of April. Ten forty, good buddy.

Not only do the seasons change in March, but the clocks do too. For reasons known only to Congress, the U.S. decided to get a jump on the Daylight Savings Time (DST) bandwagon a few years ago and moved "the change" up to the second Sunday in March, which this year is March 14. As a result, most folks will be groggy on the Ides of March this year. Beware.

Turning to astronomy, that of course, is what gives rise to the change of season from winter to spring, which rolls into town on March 20. This coincides with what we refer to as the equinox. Equinoxes separate winter from spring and summer from fall. Solstices are the boundaries between spring and summer and fall and winter.

Equinoxes and solstices are very different things. At a summer solstice, the pole gets its closest vantage point of the sun. For the northern hemisphere, this involves the North Pole and is in June, the end of spring and beginning of summer. At a winter solstice, the same pole is pointed farthest away from the sun (since the other pole at its summer solstice) and that, of course, occurs in December in the Northern Hemisphere. Equinoxes are the points halfway between the solstices and during them the two poles are exactly the same distance from the sun - neither is favored. An interesting thing occurs at that point and no, I'm not referring to balancing eggs, which is an urban legend that needs to die. Rather, on the day of the equinox, all places on Earth have 12 hours of sunshine and 12 hours of darkness.

> There is a bit of "time revolt" on the part of some locales in the U.S. Among the states, Arizona and Hawaii don't observe DST, but the Navajo Indian Reservation in Arizona does. Besides Hawaii, other island territories of the U.S. do not observe it either. These include Puerto Rico, U.S. Virgin Islands, American Samoa, Guam, and the Northern Mariana Islands. Several states, are also rumbling about making changes. They include Washington, Oregon, California, Texas, Oklahoma, and Kansas. Talk about an odd coalition (!) - DST can now be added to the list of things making for strange bedfellows.

Astronomy isn't all about us, though as there are plenty of events that have nothing to do with Earth, but we do get to watch them, making astronomy one of the best, oldest, and most widely viewed spectator sports - probably because the admission price is so low. Anyway, astronomical highlights for March include the new moon on the 13th, full moon on the 28th and half moons on the 5th and 21st. The moon and Mars will be close in the sky on 10th as will Mercury and Neptune on the 29th, but you'll never see them unless you've got a super powerful telescope needed for viewing Neptune. If not, you can celebrate National Irish-American Heritage month, Women's History Month, Celery Month, Kidney Month, Noodle Month, Frozen Food Month, and Cheerleading Safety Month. Go team!

The Odd Farmer's Almanac for 2021

March First
1912
Though many thought
The man insane
Albert Berry was first
To parachute by plane

> An Italian orthopedist is a Menditerranean

March Second
1904
The Cat in the Hat
Would soon be let loose
For today was born
Dr. Seuss

March Third
1919
From Vancouver to Seattle
Much faster than snail
Boeing was the first one
To deliver airmail

March Fourth
1877
What a splash that
It would make
When the Moscow Ballet
First performed Swan Lake

March Fifth
1956
A good day for ending
Segregation
The Supreme Court affirmed
Brown vs the Board of Education

> Miss Muffett's book
> Is out today
> The title of it?
> "Around About Whey"

March Sixth
1836
When fighting did not
Go all that well
After 13 days
The Alamo fell

March Seventh
322 BC
Philosophy
It can't be denied
Lost a lot when
Aristotle died

March Eighth
1945
In the Navy, Phyllis Daley
Became our first
African American
Service nurse

March Ninth
1964
It came out with
A mighty shine
The first Mustang off
The assembly line

March Tenth
1848
Guadaloupe-Hidalgo
A treaty you should know
Was signed to end
The war with Mexico

> My liquor store needs a good booziness plan

March Eleventh
1969
Rejoicing was heard
Among the teens
When Levis came out
With bell-bottom jeans

sidebars: "This Is Spinal Tap" released 3/2/84 · I'm so old I need a generation app · T-Rex shopped at Dinos-R-us

The Odd Farmer's Almanac for 2021

March Twelfth
1789
The Post Office today
Began it's true
And soon they'd give
Postage its due

> The Romaine empire fell when Brutus kaled Caesar

March Thirteenth
1781
William Herschel
Gave punsters insaneness
Discovering today
The planet Uranus

March Fourteenth
1794
Eli Whitney
Scored a win
Getting a patent
For the cotton gin

March Fifteenth
44 BC
The day which Brutus
Had awaited
Saw Julius Caesar
Assassinated

> The seamstress thought I was clearing my throat every time I asked her to make a hem

March Sixteenth
1850
Released today
It could not be better
Nathaniel Hawthorne's
Scarlet Letter

March Seventeenth
1905
Franklin and Eleanor
Both legendary
Showed good things can happen
When fifth cousins marry

March Eighteenth
1965
Alexei Leonov
Got cosmos rocking
When today he did
The first space walking

March Nineteenth
1918
An hour was lost
Quite by design
When Congress made
Daylight Savings Time

March Twentieth
1987
For fighting AIDS
One drug was key
The U.S. approved
AZT

March Twenty First
1908
No beverages served
The service? The worst
An airplane's passenger
Today was the first

March Twenty Second
1790
Thomas Jefferson
On this date
Became our first
Secretary of State

> Mirrorjuana - what people get high on looking at their selfies

There are many raisins for letting grapes dry out

The Jolly Green Giant is a leguminary

All Froot Loops have the same flavor

The Odd Farmer's Almanac for 2021

March Twenty Third
1857
Otis improved
Upon the dumbwaiter
Installing the first
Passenger elevator

March Twenty Fourth
1989
Polluting the sea
And damaging the soil
The Exxon Valdez
Lost a boatload of oil

March Twenty Fifth
1969
A bed-in for peace
Was novel, not loco
Credit is due
To John and Yoko

March Twenty Sixth
1827
Best known for a symphony
He called number five
This would be Beethoven's
Last morning alive

March Twenty Seventh
1884
No mention was made
Of how much it was costin'
The first long distance call
From New York to Boston

March Twenty Eighth
1979
A day when many
Sought out high land
Due to the accident
At Three Mile Island

> Guinevere was a lady of the knight

It took the creator of the Rubik's Cube, Erno Rubik, one month to solve the cube he created

> That young forest female's name will go down in nymphamy

March Twenty Ninth
1848
One of the most
Amazing of sights
Niagara Falls
Frozen in ice

March Thirtieth
1858
Hyman Lipman
The writer's friend
Patented the pencil
With an eraser on end

March Thirty First
1880
In Wabash, Indiana
They lit up the lawn
When the first electric street lights
Got turned on

Eric Idle born 3/29/1943

> The dreadful outdoor party was a fete worse than death

> "It takes considerable knowledge just to realize the extent of your own ignorance."
> – Thomas Sowell

> "The trouble with telling a good story is that it invariably reminds the other person of a dull one."
> – Sid Caesar

Page 26

Our Language Is a Funny One

Please bear with me as I recite
These lines designed perverse
Say them out loud to understand
The meaning of each verse

My uncle's says he's doing well
Although his outlook's grim
He says he will recover cuz
My antidotes on him

My neighbor's chicken's noisy
But one wolf came and then
The clucking stopped quite suddenly
I'm gladiator hen

I'll get some laughs tonight, I guess
It's been a long dry spell
The good news on the street is that
I avenue joke to tell

My brother tells the story of
When we were little dears
And got ourselves quite dirty
Then had to wash behind arrears

A giant horse fell from the barn
And made a noisy sound
But wasn't hurt at all, he landed
Forfeit on the ground

A husband goes to work to earn
His living out near Rome
But causes problems often on the
Daisies back at home

Pumped Up
The Super Bowl is over now
So football's hibernating
New England's hopes got dashed so bad
Could we say that they're deflating?

Our Language Is a Funny One

The florist down the street is bad
He is a fibbing king
Cuz I've been told this guy could almost
Lilac anything

The little baby's got it made
I think that's fair to say
Sleeps all night and poops his pants
And laziness crib all day

When I got sick, my doctor helped
He turned to me and said
"I think recovery will begin"
"The miniature back in bed"

My cat's annoying me right now
Makes noises in the moonlight
And given opportunity will
Mutilate at night

A newbie on the baseball field
Was learning it's the case
That when you hit the ball you have
Toronto the first base

If you get thirsty, worry not
There's no way you will croak
Cuz I have brought for you today
A big Canada Coke

I went away a week and I
Was certainly concerned
That everything might change
But nothing nuisance I returned

I balance up atop my head
A ball, some are aghast
But I find I must walk quite slow
It falsify move too fast

March Mudness

March Madness is March Mudness here
But everybody knows
That this is just the time of year
Preceding pollen woes

It's also when we set our clocks
And have a vernal equinox
Which means that day time equals night
So every evening's looking bright

Much longer days, more time outside
Thanks to the early dawns
We're told to all beware of ides
And look for leprechauns

Now we're in spring, the birdies sing
In Mother Nature's splendor
The sky is bright and all is right
Except for one offender

I speak of toys they call Lawn Boys
Pushed 'round by green grass growers
May I request, they reinvest
In quiet electric mowers?

Pessimistic entomologists collect katydidn'ts

Northwest Spring

Flowers bloom
And songbirds sing
As winter's gloom
Gives way to spring

Surrounding us
Are mountains tall
Powdered with
A late snowfall

On all the peaks
The tops are white
They warm our souls
And bring delight

The farmer's market
Coming soon
Portends some lazy
Afternoons

Tide pools, sand
And ocean breeze
Are therapeutic
Vitamin seas

The Hope of Spring

The sun is shining, robins sing
It cannot be too far from spring
When hope displaces dark despair
I love that more than anything

So go plant seeds that sprout and root
And let new growth reconstitute
An outlook rosy, no more dread
Let peacefulness fill up your head

And be happy

Going to Pot

On smoking marijuana, I hear it's true
Your memory goes away from you
There's just one thing. I have no clue
What does smoking marijuana do?

March 14

Today each person
My eye sees
Is of the sign
They call Pi-sces
Happy Pi Day

The Odd Farmer's Almanac for 2021

The Units Verse

Two thousand pounds of Chinese soup
Will make a restaurant run
In Beijing, China order it
In units of **Won ton**

Religious leaders measure clout
From Nome to Amsterdam
By how much sway they have with God
The units - **billi-grams**

Four fifty four graham crackers is
An awful lot to bake
Into dessert when prepping up
A really good **pound cake**

The units used for cleaning breath
Are very small, so cope
One millionth of a mouthwash is
A single **microScope**

I bet you didn't know the floor
Was there until it beckoned
You hit a peel and then went down
In one **bananosecond**

And when your mother's mother goes
To phone you from her van
Speed dialing is the way she calls
That is one **instagram**

A nickel isn't worth too much
In these inflated times
Put four of them together
To make a **paradigms**

And then there's laryngitis
When speaking goes all sour
You know that you can measure it
In units of **hoarsepower**

I hate it when my socks get wet
It's not what I'd have chosen
A thousand milliliters of
Them make one **literhosen**

The Units Verse

For mockingbirds two thousand is
A lot, please hear my words
But that's what you will need to have
Two **kilomockingbirds**

And if you shuffle playing cards
Remember fifty two
Is what you have when someone hands
One **decacard** to you

A tiny trout, I just found out
Won't make a tasty dish
Cuz one millionth of one of those
Is just a **microfiche**

And if you're into monogramming
Listen to me, ma'am
A pair of them together gives
One single **diagram**

If you should lose your voice it might
Just leave you feeling sour
But think of it in better terms
You've now got more **hoarse power**

A unit that I really like
Is for drinking low-cal beer
Three hundred sixty five days of that
Corresponds to one **Lite year**

I used to watch The Twilight Zone
It left my head a-swirling
Sixteen point five feet of film from it
Is the same as one **Rod Serling**

Now, when it comes to thinking
I think that you will find
The unit of a dimwit
Is called a half a mind

And if that leaves you groaning
Get ready - it gets worse
One million things left aching
Is just one **mega-hertz**

What do anxious butterflies get in their stomachs?

The Units Verse

Hey don't quit now, because I am
Starting to get rollin'
A half of an intestine
Is called a **semi-colon**

OK, I'll close, reminding folks
Who are geometrically inclined
The shortest distance 'tween two jokes
Is always one **straight line**

Some Thoughts on Elon Musk

Elon Musk put his car in space
I find the idea comical
And even worse, I'm sure it's true
Insurance is astronomical

When it comes to putting cars in space
Musk knows how to talk it
His heavy lifting launch will mean
More dollars in his pocket
I'd guess that Teslas now will see
Their prices all skyrocket

Twinkle little star so faint
You're way out there, but I sure ain't
The Tesla headed where you are
Made Elon ask "Dude, where's my car?"

If Elon Musk has trouble great
I think he'd best beware
His scandal they'll call Elongate
A long drawn out affair

Charge!

A ruler saw
Electric prices
Rising high for sure
So now they're free
For everyone
And he's an amperer

"You can't have everything. Where would you put it?" - Steven Wright

Shorties

Getting Steamed
I learned today
From plumber Bob
On-demand hot water
Is a tankless job

Fly's Cracker
The fly o'er there
On that Triscuit
Put all her eggs
In one biscuit

Mooving Livestock
To buy a cow
Farmer Boggs
Goes and looks
In cattle-ogs

Side Story
I wanted a square
To build upon
But cut corners and got
An octagon

Misdeal
The lady says she's
Thinking hard
But her deck is missing
Several cards

Filthy Language
The mother cried,
"This is insanity"
"Your dirt's a grime"
"Against humanity"

Monitor the Situation
I broke my Dell
It was so easy
Shattered into
Bits and PCs

Picking Locks
I need to go back
On my meds
My Jamaican hairstyle
Left me with dreads

The Odd Farmer's Almanac for 2021

Shorties

Eye Onic
What does salt
To water do?
It simply says
"I solute you"

Getting Lit
Chemotherapy's
Ugly ills
Remind us all
Smoking kills

Floored
A dog I saw
Just left me nervous
It made the floor
A pup lick surface

Sir Cuitous
Medieval armor
To my delight
Got shipped to me
Over knight

Mapped Out
Geology studies
Rocks most flat
But geography
Is where it's at

Red, He Said
The communist who is
Spewing venom
Is airing out
His dirty Lenin

Bottled Up
The peanut said
With just a sniff
"I'll be back"
"In a Jif"

Shorties

Getting Started
A doorman has
Just one mission
In his entry
Level position

More Double Meanings

An **arbitrator** settles things
Between two dueling Ronalds
But also is a cook who moves
From Arby's to McDonald's

Ms **Bernadette's** a lass who brings
A song onto the stage
But also what one does when we
Have paid up our mortgage

Heroes are brave people who
Stood tall though danger was
And also what an oarsman in
A boat race often does

The **parasites** infecting things
Make healthy people cower
And also are what people see
When on the Eiffel Tower

A **pharmacist** gives medicine
To help ease your alarm
And also what you do if you
Go help out on the farm

Sunglasses help to **polarize**
The light that's coming through
And also are the things with which
A big white bear sees you

Risque talk is bawdy shaming

What's another word for 'thesaurus'?

Spanish flu is caused by junk email

"When I hear somebody sigh, 'Life is hard,' I am always tempted to ask, 'Compared to what?'" - Sydney J. Harris

Fizzics - the only degree offered at Alka Seltzer U

The Odd Farmer's Almanac for 2021

APRIL 2021

With the excitement of National Noodle month behind us, we leap forward to April, the first month of the year with 30 days. Why, you may wonder, do the months vary as they do in their number of days? Thankfully, for the space I have to fill here, the answer is not a simple one. The Roman calendar originally had 10 months of varying lengths starting in March and ending in December. Winter, which now includes January and February, didn't have months back then. That wreaked havoc on collecting bills for cable TV, so in 713 BC, King Pompilius added January and February and the latter had varying numbers of days. When Julius Caesar instituted the cleverly named Julian calendar, he decreed months would alternate between 30 and 31 days. Making the 4th (April), 6th (June), 9th (September) and 11th (November) months be alternating is probably something only an emperor could understand (or get away with). By the way, April originally had 29 days and only got its thirtieth day with the introduction of the Gregorian calendar in 1582.

> We don't really know where the name "April" came for the month. One idea is from Latin where it is claimed the word 'aperire' gave rise to Aprilis, meaning "to open," as flowers and trees do at this time of the year. Another thought is that April comes from Aphrilis, which derives from Aphrodite, the goddess of what 90% of nature appears to be in at this time of year.

> The Easter Bunny is one of the odder traditions associated with religious holidays (the red suited, bearded North Pole dweller with flying reindeer is a close second). It appears to have come with German immigrants to Pennsylvania in the 1700s who celebrated a traditional "Osterhase" - an egg laying rabbit. The belief multiplied like, um, rabbits, giving us a religious experience we can all enjoy - chocolate Easter bunnies.

April is best known for its showers, its fools, and its taxes, not necessarily in order of significance. It's also the month that major league baseball gets into full swing (har!) and the NBA and NHL begin plodding through their interminable playoffs. Bingo anyone?

April is also the time of year when the thoughts of about 90% of nature turn to "love" or whatever you want to call it. Chirping, strutting, nest building, and singles ads all peak this month. You have to wonder why they didn't put Valentine's Day in April. But I digress.

April is also a common month for lunar religious observations. Christians celebrate Easter on April 4 (Sunday after the first full moon after March 21), Muslims begin Ramadan on April 13th (1st day of the ninth month of the Islamic lunar calendar) and Jews end Passover on the 4th as well. Because the 29 day lunar cycle does not divide 365 day years evenly, dates of lunar holidays vary from year to year.

Up in the sky, you can see either April showers or, if it is not raining on the 22nd, the Lyrid meteor showers. The moon is halved on the 4th and 19th, new on the 11th, and full on the 26th. It also appears close to Saturn on the 6th and Jupiter on the 7th.

The Odd Farmer's Almanac for 2021

April First
1778
Oliver Pollock
On his hands had much time
So he sat and invented
The dollar sign

April Second
1931
Jackie Mitchell is a woman
You may not know her name
But she struck out Ruth and Gehrig
In an exhibition game

April Third
1860
From Missouri to California
It was a great success
Delivering the mail
Via Pony Express

April Fourth
1581
Today in England
They celebrated
When Sir Francis Drake
Circumnavigated

> A non-functioning skunk is out of odor

April Fifth
1792
Though Congress didn't
Think it so neato
George Washington cast
The very first veto

April Sixth
1909
Peary and Henson
With a long icy stroll
Became the first ones
To reach the North Pole

> People who die for low prices are known as Walmartyrs

A duel between three people is actually called a truel

April Seventh
1933
The dry spell now was over
A long time it had been
Happy days for all beer drinkers
It was legal once again

April Eighth
1974
He broke Babe Ruth's record
No steroids - all clean
When Hank Aaron hit
Number seven fifteen

April Ninth
1970
The world to the news
On this day was woken up
To learn that the Beatles
Had just broken up

April Tenth
1912
As maiden voyages go
Some are more groovy
This one by Titanic
Led to a big movie

April Eleventh
1814
Able was he
A remarkable fella
Napolean abdicated
Exiled to Elba

"War is God's way of teaching Americans geography." - Ambrose Bierce

> "Facebook sounds like a drag. In my day seeing pictures of people's vacations was considered a punishment."
> – Betty White

Page 33

The Odd Farmer's Almanac for 2021

April Twelfth
1955
An important event
On the medical scene
Jonas Salk announced
A polio vaccine

April Thirteenth
1970
In the biggest detour
The world's ever seen
A big change of plans
For Apollo 13

April Fourteenth
1912
Titanic discovered
By hitting ice blocks
A rather sad meaning
To the phrase "on the rocks"

> In barber college, cutting class is essential

Wheels are highway rubbery

April Fifteenth
1955
Now it is a day
Nutritionists rue
The McDonalds era
Begins for fast food

April Sixteenth
1972
Ping-pong opened China
To our foreign affairs
And the next step today
Was two panda bears

> Mansplaining is correctile dysfunction

Counter refinishers get paid for surfaces rendered

April Seventeenth
1929
Babe Ruth was a powerful hitter
Who also was great when he pitched
And today to Ms Claire Hodgson
The Bambino got hitched

April Eighteenth
1908
8.25 Richters
Are very serious earthquakes
And with that, San Francisco
Came down with a case of the shakes

April Nineteenth
1982
Sally Ride rode a rocket
Into space, it was sweet
Calling astronauts men
Was now obsolete

> Velcro is a ripoff

April Twentieth
1770
Though his plans in Hawaii
Would be thrown asunder
Captain Cook today
Found Australia down under

After 20 years of leading an insect aerobics class, I'm still working out all the bugs

April Twenty First
1862
The most valuable things
Are what they misprint
Starting today
The U.S. Mint

> "Be careful about reading health books. You may die of a misprint."
> – Mark Twain

Page 34

The Odd Farmer's Almanac for 2021

> "You're my rock"
> is a polite way of saying
> "I take you for granite"

April Twenty Second
1889
In a classic case
Of supply and demand
Thousands of settlers
Claimed Oklahoma land

April Twenty Third
1896
Though there was no red carpet
The significance was clear
When the first motion picture
Had its New York premiere

April Twenty Fourth
1981
The first of many million
Crashes would be
Arising from
The IBM-PC

April Twenty Fifth
1953
The twists and the turns
Of genetics today
Came from Watson and Crick's
Structure of DNA

> Vacation bills remind you
> to cut down on suites

April Twenty Sixth
1986
Cold winter nights
In an old Russian town
Would ne'er be the same
When Chernobyl melted down

April Twenty Seventh
1509
Considering them
A Vatican menace
The Pope excommunicated
The city of Venice

April Twenty Eighth
1947
Riding a boat
That likely was leaky
Heyerdahl piloted
The raft called Kon Tiki

April Twenty Ninth
1852
If you need a word
For a brontosaurus
The place find it
Roget's Thesaurus

April Thirtieth
1803
A massive land mass
From the south to Montana
Came our way in a purchase
Dubbed Louisiana

> People who worship paper bags
> are sack religious

"The road to success is always under construction" - Lily Tomlin

"If you can't live without me, why aren't you dead already?" - Cynthia Heimel

"If life was fair, Elvis would be alive and all the impersonators would be dead."
– Johnny Carson

"Things will get better --
despite our efforts
to improve them"
- Will Rogers

Page 35

In the Big Inning

In the big inning God did create
A pentagon he called home plate
And there upon it where he stood
God declared it "Verily, good"

And it was

Around what God called infield spaces
He scattered there a set of bases
And put three players guarding them
The first and second and third base men

Next he built the outfield walls
And created shortstops fielding balls
Then further back and oh so deft
God put outfielders - right, center, left

To get the games up fast and going
He set catchers catching and pitchers throwing
And seeing what they did to hitters
God said "Thou shalt not throw spitters"

But many broke his commandment

And while it was a major boner
God spent time creating owners
He stipulated one condition
That umps would make the games' decisions

And arguments were born

That too was fine for many years
But later God would shift his gears
He didn't like a call one day
And so invented instant replay

The Almighty wasn't all controllin'
No punishment for bases stolen
Four balls did God declare a walk
And hesitation was a balk

The Odd Farmer's Almanac for 2021

In the Big Inning

Although it made the pitchers groan
He set a fairly small strike zone
And limiting the hitters' clout
God said three strikes should be an out

Unless the catcher dropped the ball

Where there was flatness on the ground
God created the pitcher's mound
But said it shouldn't be too high
Six inches upwards toward the sky

And God said scorers would be ones
Who circled bases, making runs
To keep employed statistics guys
God created RBIs

And the clean up hitter was born

For keeping balance, God gave ways
To get two outs with double plays
And three outs God an inning made
Then after nine of them were played
He said the team that won a game
Would have more runs beside its name

But if no team by nine was winning
A game would go to extra innings
Visualizing what this portends
God made relief pitchers for the ends

And in the 7th innings, God stretched

With insightfulness he had so vast
God put the home teams batting last
And trying hard to make things better
God came up with the double header

A different decision made folks bitter
Involving designated hitters
The fighting caused in God fatigue
So he said, "Just for the American League"

Mooning is to me too much luna, see?

Inuit Valentine - "I only have ice for you"

Under table footsie is just play toe

The Odd Farmer's Almanac for 2021

In the Big Inning

And the All Star game and the World Series

Each league began with just eight teams
Til God let down his guard, it seems
So Satan took advantage and
Declared expansion 'cross the land

And God said, "Uh oh"

Expansion plans spread teams around
And took them out of Polo Grounds
Today the remnants of these ways
Are with us now as Devil Rays

Of course

And owner greed and tough contracts
Burned Ruth and Gehrig and Sandy Koufax
So when Curt Flood said that he'd been screwed
Claiming indentured servitude
God the almighty did agree
And thus was born free agency

Look what happened to that

Next in the land, there soon arose
A problem everybody knows
Performance enhancing drugs became
A lot more than a bedroom game
New kinds of cheating, now well known
Those muscle building male hormones

And you-know-who was behind this

Finally God with a giant frown
Put his most almighty foot down
He said, "I'm announcing here today"
"We'll start by having interleague play"
"And to finally atone for the O'Leary's"
"He let the Cubbies win a Series"

And things got better across the land

My diet doctor's one word advice: "Fondon't"

Puncil - what I use to write funnies

Fishermen need angler management classes

Page 38

The Odd Farmer's Almanac for 2021

April Sours

The Easter bunny left some sweets
They said in Sunday School
But when we went to find his treats
They cried out, "April Fools!"

The warmth's returning to the north
As flowers from their beds burst forth
Songbirds are building nests in trees
And we're at the end of flu disease

It is the time when springtime shows us
Garden beds of lovely roses
Then for beauty we can all depend on
Enormous blooms of rhododendrons

But let us not forget that spring
Leaves many folks crestfallen
They dread the song that nature sings
To them, it's quite 'a pollen'

But as the month takes its final bow
Our attitudes have soured
Instead of spring and everything
April simply showered

The Preying Mantis

A male preying mantis
Drinking in a bar
Says that he doesn't wanna
Get into his car

Doesn't wanna walk
Doesn't wanna roam
His wife'll bite his head off
As soon as he gets home

> "The safe way to double your money is to fold it over once and put it in your pocket." - Kin Hubbard

Shorties

Hanes' Stains
Edible underwear's
Getting quirky
Now they're making
New brief jerky

Lettuce Have More
The grocer loudly
Just complained
There's no more lettuce
That romained

Curdeous
The cheese shop owner
Has odd views
He says he's happy
With the bleus

Getting a Buzz
To bees, a hive
Is like a dormA
They stay in winter
Cuz 'swarm

Wench Warmer
The medical advice
Of which I'm sure
Is to keep a uterus
At womb temperature

Stepping Up
It rang quite true
To those in attendance
The inventor of stairs
Had many descendents

No Noose is Good Noose
I suppose there are
Folks who whine
'Bout hangmen working
Under dead lines

A Playtex on the clothesline in the sun is hanging out in bra daylight

Women Scientists
(for Chelsea)

Rosalind Franklin toiled away
While probing forms of DNA
Then Watson Crick without a song
Observed her data, that was wrong

They got full credit no surprise
And won a fifties Nobel Prize
Then Barb McClintock doing screens
Discovered maize's jumping genes

They said she was off her rocker
Genes don't move, many mocked her
But detractors made a major gaffe
And Barbara lived to have a laugh

You see she had more wisdom
Than simple minded cretins
That's why she got the biggest prize
They give in Stockholm Sweden

The Windows® guy was a real pane

Circular Logic

I don't think
I have the willpower
For a diet

I don't think
I can change things
Why try it?

I don't think
My vote
Will count

I don't think
Things improve
On my account

I don't think

Phone Follies

I was feeling blue just yesterday
Til I dialed a corporation
The automated voice I got
Began a conversation

Its perky tone raised up my hopes
An automated gem
It told me that my call was very
Important to all of them

And that feeling of importance soared
With the voice's reassurance
That my call would be recorded for
Quality assurance

I guess they think me knowledgeable
In all the things I say
My spirits buoyed I walked around
On a cloud the rest of the day

There's just one thing that puzzles me
And it is rather strange
Why is it every time I call
The menu options change?

Merry Mary

Mary had a little lamb
It was a tasty dish
And after Mary ate the lamb
She craved a bit of fish

The fish was very yummy but
She needed to exert
Instead she toodled off to get
A very big dessert

Oh please don't be like Mary
Avoid big piles of fries
Unless you think that it is grand
Supersizing thighs

The Odd Farmer's Almanac for 2021

MAY 2021

April showers bring May flowers and May flowers bring . . . . . pollen, pilgrim. Anyone who lives here in the Willamette Valley of Oregon knows all about this - windshields covered with the yellow stuff and clouds of it hovering over the thousands of acres of grass seed farms covering the valley. Growing grass for seed is a big cash crop in Western Oregon and yes, I'm talking about the yard stuff, not the plant whose profits go "up in smoke." There's plenty of that too in Oregon and it's a big money maker - legal now, to boot -YAY! Oregon's far from alone in this regard, with the list of states decriminalizing, permitting medical use, or recreational use growing all the time. But there I go digressing again.*

> As The Odd Farmer's Almanac was going to press, there are only 8 states that had not at least decriminalized or allowed possession for medical purposes of the evil weed - Wisconsin, Tennessee, Alabama, South Carolina, Idaho, Wyoming, South Dakota, and Kansas.

The first day of May is often referred to as May Day and it is the day on which most of the non-U.S. world celebrates Labor Day. May Day is also associated with the Maypole, which itself is linked to European pagan dancing in the Middle Ages. The dance, which is a celebration of fertility, involves a lot of fun and frolicking, which meant, of course, that it was scandalous at various points in history. The British Parliament banned Maypole dancing in 1644 after Oliver Cromwell described it as "a Heathenish vanity, generally abused to superstition and wickedness."

Though we associate May Day today with happiness, the expression "mayday, mayday, mayday" (note the joining of the words) is used to declare dangerous situations. Why? Turns out, the 'mayday' comes from the convergence of radio transmission and flying. In the 1920s, air traffic over the English Channel spiked along with corresponding problems. Pilots needed a clear way to communicate they needed help. Radio-based telegraphy on ships used three dots, three dashes, and three dots - S.O.S. The problem with the letter 'S' when spoken, though, is that it sounds like 'F'. A voice-based transmission of SOS might thus be misunderstood, so an alternative was sought. The expression 'mayday' repeated three times was chosen for two reasons. First, it didn't sound like anything else and second, it had roots in the French phrase 'm'aider,' which translates as 'help me.' Frederick Stanley Mockford, a senior British radio officer, is given unsubstantiated credit for coming up with the phrase. It also made him unsubstantiatedly famous, which may be why you've never heard of him.

Air travel moves attention upwards and reminds this writer that he'd better get the month's astronomical forecast together before running out of space (HAR!). The moon is the usual star (HAR!) of the show going from half to new to half to full on the 3rd, 11th, 19th, and 26th respectively. A total lunar eclipse gets thrown in on the 26th. The moon cuddles up to Saturn on the 3rd and Jupiter on the 4th. Venus and Mercury do the same on the 28th and the moon, never one to give up easily, makes another close pass by Saturn on the 30th. With that, I happily conclude this column before running out of spac

*I have been diagnosed as being "passive digressive"

The Odd Farmer's Almanac for 2021

May First
1486
Christopher Columbus
A wee bit confused
Got Isabella to fund
A West Indies cruise

> Two appliances shrink clothes - dryers and refrigerators

May Second
1903
Benjamin Spock today began
Infancy with a hook
The experience that he had in it
He turned into a book

Plants have all the anthers

May Third
1978
A massive email message
Went out just as programmed
The recipients of it didn't know
That they were the first ones spammed

May Fourth
1961
Civil rights activists in the south
Had quite a long list of insiders
Thirteen of them on a bus this day
Were called the Freedom Riders

> Ocean organisms with biting humor are sharkastic

May Fifth
1961
Alan Shepard took a ride
Up to the edge of space
Looking down he realized
He'd flown all over the place

May Sixth
1994
Trains connecting England and France
Are certainly appealing
"Chunnel" riders can experience now
A brand new sinking feeling

May Seventh
1789
George Washington
Standing tall
Had the first
Inaugural Ball

May Eighth
1886
John Pemberton
Hit payola
Coming up with
Coca Cola

"If you must make a noise, make it quietly"- Oliver Hardy

May Ninth
1864
"They couldn't hit an elephant at this dist . . "
Is what General Sedgwick said
The words are notable today because
A bullet then killed him dead

May Tenth
1960
The USS Nautilus
A submarine sensation
Completed the first underwater
Circumnavigation

> The difference between sleeping and awake states is eye-opening

> "I like long walks, especially when they are taken by people who annoy me."
> —Noel Coward

Page 42

The Odd Farmer's Almanac for 2021

Alimony is bounty on the mutiny

May Eleventh
1502
Columbus sought India
On his fourth voyage today
But just as happened thrice before
America got in his way

May Twelfth
1938
Anticipating the 60s
That no one could foresee
Sandoz Labs
Started making LSD

May Thirteenth
1846
War on Mexico!
That was the plan
Declared just two months
After fighting began

May Fourteenth
1853
The inventor Gail Borden
With patenting, commenced
The making of milk
That was fully condensed

May Fifteenth
1930
Ellen Church
Met success
As the world's first
Stewardess

May Sixteenth
1866
A man named Charles Hire
Whom soda drinkers revere
Went out and invented
His brand of root beer

George Carlin born 5/12/1937

"Chaotic action is preferable to orderly inaction" - Will Rogers

The dog's itching problem was a fleasco

May Seventeenth
1900
Receiving a round
Of thunderous applause
L. Frank Baum published
"The Wonderful Wizard of Oz"

May Eighteenth
1652
An act at the time
Of considerable bravery
Rhode Island outlawed
The practice of slavery

May Nineteenth
1971
The USSR
Looking up to the stars
Launched a new spacecraft
But it collided with Mars

May Twentieth
1899
The first speeding ticket
Turned a cabbie's day sour
Recklessly driving
At 12 miles per hour

Italy's Big Foot is known as "Spagyeti"

May Twenty First
1927
Flying all day
And all through the night
Lindbergh completed
His big solo flight

Old age is when actions creak louder than words

"Trying is the first step toward failure" - Homer Simpson

Page 43

The Odd Farmer's Almanac for 2021

> The talking pine tree was amazing, needles to say

May Twenty Second
1908
Orville and Wilbur
New on the scene
Patented what they called
A "flying machine"

May Twenty Third
1618
The Thirty Years War
Was rather sublime
It started today
And ended on time

May Twenty Fourth
1844
Samuel Morse
Quite inspired
Today for the first time
Found himself wired

May Twenty Fifth
585 BC
Loose lips sink ships
The pundit quips
But today Thales used them
To predict the first eclipse

May Twenty Sixth
1977
A long time ago
In a galaxy far away
Star Wars began
On this very day

May Twenty Seventh
1647
Achsah Young
Thanks to a snitch
Was the first executed
Massachusetts witch

May Twenty Eighth
1937
Then, like now
There was a wait
When the first cars crossed
The Golden Gate

May Twenty Ninth
1953
Hillary and Norgay
Got what they did seek
The highest point on
Mt. Everest's peak

May Thirtieth
1431
One of Europe's
Greatest names
Joan of Arc
Went up in flames

May Thirty First
1902
Though it certainly was
Very well attended
A Boer-ing war
On this day ended

"If you're going through hell, keep going" - Winston Churchill

"The road to success is dotted with many tempting parking spaces - Will Rogers

> A golddigger is a will-oiled machine

"Laughing at our mistakes
can lengthen our own life.
Laughing at someone else's
can shorten it."
– Cullen Hightower

"If you could kick the person in
the pants responsible for most
of your trouble,
you wouldn't sit for a month."
– Theodore Roosevelt

The Odd Farmer's Almanac for 2021

An Ode to May

May the 4th be with you all
We heard just days ago
From Star Wars hipsters big and small
And others in the know

Out in the yard, the noise I hear
Is splishing with some sploshing
That only means one thing, it's clear
My neighbor's power washing

I'm puzzled by the need to use
A very strengthened squirt
Is it the case someone's confused
A stain for power dirt?

Though it's an odd phenomenon
I guess I'll let it ride
At least it's not like chewing on
Those power pods of Tide

May also is the time when Greeks
Lost one of their greatest movers
Twas in this month that Socrates
Invented the Hemlock Maneuver

And one last wish to close this rhyme
I hope it's not too dreary
Oh please let graduation time
Be when it's partly cleary

An Ode to Mae

A flower in
The forest grew
Its color no one
Ever knew

The form it took
We do not know
How long it lived
Where did it grow?

If there's no ears
When elm trees fall
It's said they make
No sound at all

Of flowers one has
Never thought
Did they exist?
Some say they'd not

So I say
Most ecstatically
I'm happy you
Have thought of me

Graduation

So it is graduation day
A time that once seemed far away
Now after this hip hip hooray
It's time to do your thing

We all await your expertise
Some educated strategies
The world is yours, here are the keys
They'll open anything

The Daily Grind

The alarm clock rings
I rub my eyes
Roll out of bed
The night time flies

A world of dreams
Is left behind.
I long now for
The daily grind

It's not my work
I'm talking 'bout
It's coffee and
WHY THE HELL ARE WE OUT?

2019 Obituaries

"One white, one black, one blonde"
Fought crime on our TVs
For Mod Squad's lovely Peggy
It was a Lipton tease

Peter Mayhew, known as Chewie
You're gone, we shed a tear
A member of the Star Wars crewie
Once named Wookie of the Year

Doris Day has gone away
Goodbye Rodeo drive
I feel untracked. How to react?
Didn't know she was alive

Eddie Money
Paid the price
Used half his tickets
To paradise

On her own terms
Life to the hilt
That is what
Gloria Vanderbilt

"Verry interesting," so would say
The Johnson known as Arte
The reason he's not here today?
Failure of his hearty

By being in the Right Place
Doc John saw his fame climb
His music never missed a beat
But his heart was in the Wrong Time

Wild Kingdom host and naturalist
Jim Fowler now is dead
The animals, he could not resist
"Twas Mutual," they said

Louisa Moritz, aged seventy two
The now dead actress was
Notable quite famously
For implicating Cos

Tesla, SpaceX, and HyperLoop are three Musk tiers

Nike operates on a shoestring budget

2019 Obituaries

Bill Buckner was an All-Star who
Unfortunately made his name
Not for outstanding playing
But one bad Series game

With Mickey, Mike and Davy
He was a 60s whiz
Now Peter Tork has gone away
No more Monkee biz

Peter Fonda gone da way
Of his late father Henry
His star flared Easy Rider bright
Then went out in his 70s

I craved a house from I.M. Pei
They looked so very nice
But I would never get one cuz
He asked too high a Preice

Sherlock Holmes

When Sherlock Holmes
Went up to Boston
His sidekick rode along

Driving up there
In a Datsun
The trip was very long

When they saw a citrus
In the sun
Sidekick said, "That's wrong"

Said Sherlock.
"It's a lemon tree, dear Watson,"
"Now please just move along"

Shouldn't drug store helpers be called Pharmacistants?

> "I was married by a judge. I should have asked for a jury."
> – Groucho Marx

Page 46

The Odd Farmer's Almanac for 2021

Sports Team Names

I'm guessing not many screams and shouts
For the Belgian team the **Brussels Sprouts**

The other Belgian team is awful
Their fans call them the **Belgium Waffles**

And down in France, they all prefer
To be rooting for the **Cannes Openers**

In the Philippines, the fans are bolder
Than their team is, the **Manila Folders**

In Prague the team is known as trouncers
They are called the big **Czech Bouncers**

The other Prague team you might resist
Cuz they're the **Prague Topologists**

In Baghdad, Beatles fans all swoon
For the local team, the **Iraqi Raccoons**

Koreans sometimes take their dates
To go and cheer on their own **Seoul Mates**

The Taiwan team, in actuality
Dominates - the **Taipei Personalities**

In Venezuela, demonstrations
When they win - **Caracus Celebrations**

For the Romanian team, winning looms
Number one - the **Bucharest Rooms**

A Texas team will never cower
They say baby, they're the **Austin Powers**

And out in Italy a grassy grower
Will likely "root" for the **Milan Mowers**

The Caribbean team I'm prone to guess
Has moms who ask, "**Jamaica Mess**?"

In the Atlantic island any team that tangles
Gets lost playing the **Bermuda Triangles**

In Ireland, they cheer when their team wins
Yelling for the **Dublin Mint Twins**

Sports Team Names

In Russia, fans are awfully batty
Cheering for the **Moscow Patties**

The Alaska team has no weekend play
Cuz they're the **Fairbanks Holidays**

And don't forget in U of O nation
Their numero uno, the **Eugene Mutations**

The Beatle's hometown fans most able
Like rooting for the **Liverpool Tables**

In Budapest, each fan will back
The team they call the **Hungary Jacks**

And in Holland, the Dutch are pleased
To pull for the **Amsterdam Yankees**

A Georgia team has many groupies
I'm referring to the **Macon Whoopies**

Their other team is somewhat older
They're the **Budapest Controllers**

Nevadans cheer with lots of verve
Their team of teams, the **Las Vegas Nerves**

A gritty team with taste most awful
Is known as the **San Diego Waffles**

In South Carolina, fans say the answer
Is their team the **Charleston Dancers**

The Wisconsin team's fans are very cocky
When they pull for the **Milwaukee Talkies**

And out on eastern Washington's plains
You'll be a fan of **Yakima Chains**

In rural Alaska, every Aleut sees
Their favorites there, the **Nome Chomskis**

In Minnesota it's the truth
Dentists cheer for **Duluth Tooths**

Some Illinois fans with thinning dreams
Cheer loudly for the **Moline Cuisines**

Sports Team Names

In Germany, fans all get their jollies
Rooting for the **Leipzig Field Follies**

In Lebanon, fans who feel the pulse
Cheer for the **Beirut Vegetables**

And in the South, fans in attendance
Rely on **New Mexico Dependents**

On Vancouver Island, winning plans
Are made by **Victoria's Secret** fans

And though their team is in the basement
Aussies Docs cheer **Sydney Replacements**

While island life can be a repressor
It's not for fans of the **Tonga Depressors**

And what about those Irish hawkers
Following the **Belfast Talkers?**

In Nevada, they say nobody bickers
About the **Carson City Slickers**

And build your antibiotic collection
If you follow the **Flagstaff Infections**

Mississippi fans will not heap scorn on
Their confusing team, the **Beloxi Morons**

Though some New Yorkers have bad habits
In the capitol they're **Albany Rabbits**

Pennsylvania fans take chances
Following the **Erie Circumstances**

The British fans make many squeals
Cheering for the **Essex Appeals**

Another British team used to bite
I'm referring to the **Exeter Mites**

For one sports team, it's only fair
To say they stink - **Londonderry Airs**

Sports Team Names

Australian fans root for the catcher
You see, their team is the **Perth Snatchers**

In Ethiopia, tix aren't cheap
To watch the **Addis Ababa Black Sheep**

No need to be in a hurry folks
If you plan to watch the **Oslo Pokes**

A Wheel of Fortune mascot's right
For a team that's called the **Havana Whites**

And one team that strives for sex appeal
Is Pennsylvania's **Lehigh Heels**

It's sad to think there's double deckers
Cheering on the **Stockholm Wreckers**

And fans of midgets very wise
Will cheer for France's **Lisle Bitty Guys**

But be careful to avoid the hole
Of the team they call the **Selma Souls**

I wonder what would be the score
If Selma played the **Christchurch Goers**

And SNL fans on Saturdays
Go watch their team, the **Argentina Phase**

A hungry Alabaman never bitches
They go see the **Birmingham Sandwiches**

But I don't think a team's name's badder
Than the one called the **Senegal Bladders**

And do you suppose there's early arrivers
To watch the **Madagascar Drivers?**

In La Paz a fan almost never yawns
Rooting for the **Bolivia Newton Johns**

British bathrooms are occupied by loo tenants

The Odd Farmer's Almanac for 2021

Books at the Library

The library says that it has stocked
New books for its book lovers
The titles shouldn't leave you shocked
Let's go there and discover

The first is "*How to Write Big Books*"
It is a new release
The author who created it?
His name is Warren Peace

"*The Argument Resolution Book*"
Is brilliant and it's deft
I congratulate the man who wrote it
He goes by Xavier Breath

An adventure book, "*The Lion Attacked*"
Is one I think of oft
A writer spent much time on it
We thank you Claude Yarmoff

And "*All the Favorite Children's Songs*"
May put you fast asleep
The lady who compiled them all
Was Barbara Blacksheep

If "*Positive Reinforcement*" is
The thing you need, please know
The author worked on it quite hard
Let's thank him, Wade Ago

"*School Truancy*" is long to read
But it is time well spent
Or so its author said to us
His name? Marcus Absent

"*The Indian Cloakroom Attendant*" book
Is clever. It gets my vote
As the best short story I have read
By the author Mahatma Coat

If you're looking for "*Some Party Fun*"
On this topic many grapple
Until they find the book that's by
The man called Bob Frapples

Books at the Library

If you aspire to "*Archery*"
Be careful, there is peril
As you will learn by reading from
The book by Beau N. Arrow

I hope you will not think that
"*Irish Heart Surgery*" is too nasty
The author is a specialist
Dr. Angie O'Plasty

"*The Philippine Post Office*" book
Is good, there's nothing better
The author's from Manila and
Her name's Imelda Letter

And finally "*I Hurt Myself*"
Was written by two clowns
Who do slapstick. Their pseudonyms
Are Eileen Dover and Phil Down

Utopia

You have a world
Comprised of friends
Who like when you're happy
Who admire all you do
Who love you
And are with you on every move

Your world is perfect
Your movies fluid
Your pictures sharp
Your music apt
All problems gone

You made this world
In your own image
And the only thing in it
More powerful than you
Is the smart phone you used to create it

Jimmy Hoffa's murder won't be solved without concrete evidence

The Odd Farmer's Almanac for 2021

JUNE 2021

June is the month of cycles. By now, you hopefully have recovered from the Mayhem (HAR!) of Memorial Day festivities and are midway through the repetitive activities of watering, cursing, and mowing the green stuff in front of and behind your house. If this year is typical, the cycle will be repeated a good 20 or so times before the growing season ends, varied only by the occasional act of edging and interrupted by the ritual of the annual family vacation. When people talk about "getting away from it all," they are often referring to grass, which is why beaches are so popular.

Lawns are the only battlegrounds where armies dare not tread, lest they trample the grass upon it. Peace on Earth would be real if the money that went to generals was given instead to lawn growers, though different kinds of battles would break out, given suburban competitiveness. Unlike the rest of the biological sciences, in the sport of Homeowner Botany, having the tallest, most biodiverse lawn is frowned up. Similarly, although "pet fertilization" is a simple, natural, and low-cost prescription for healthy grass, champions in the lawn sweepstakes eschew bio-organic treatments, dancing instead to the somnolent tune of "Weed and Feed." Two, four indeed!

June also typically marks the five month anniversary of having given up on one's new year's resolutions. Celebrants mark the occasion with a kegger and non-drinkers may instead consume cheesecake. There's plenty of opportunity to down lots of both, given that the longest day of the year hits on the 20th and this also officially opens Picnic Season, a time when the nation's picnic tables, campgrounds, and blankets emerge from their long winter sleep to discover that fat people are once again sitting, standing, and/or lying upon them. With fat people come cupcakes and with cupcakes come ants and ants always come out at picnics, thus completing what biologists know is one of the most important cycles of nature.

The last cycle of this month is the start of the annual Christmas shopping season and the countdown of the number of days left until the after-Christmas sales and post-holiday depression begin. If you hurry, you can wrap up (HAR!) your Christmas shopping by Labor Day and smugly tell all your friends. This is a good idea because it will give them enough time to forget their hatred of you by the time they are buying your prezzies - when the shopping countdown has moved to the single digits. God Rest Ye Merry Gentile Men.

Before the monthly update of astronomical cycles, I want to remind everyone that June is Black Lives Matter (BLM) month. Though I joke a lot in these spaces, BLM is an important cause worthy of everyone's attention. On a lighter note, June is also turkey leftovers month, which is very disturbing given the 7 month lag between Thanksgiving and June. Caution is advised. Astronomically, the pattern of the moon going through another set of what we politely call "phases" continues this month. They include halves on the 2nd and 17th, fullness on the 24th and newness capped with an annular eclipse on the 10th, visible in Russia, Greenland, and northern Canada. La Luna dances with the planets on the 1st (Jupiter), 13th (Mars), 27th (Saturn), and 28th (Jupiter). June also has two meteor showers - on the 10th (Aretids - unfortunately during the day) and the 27th (Bootids). Enjoy your leftovers :-)

The Odd Farmer's Almanac for 2021

June First
1533
Anne Boleyn was crowned today
If smart she'd not have wedded
But Henry the 8th controlled the path
That she would soon be headed

June Second
1910
Charles Stewart Rolls flew a plane
'Cross the English Channel both ways
But was England's first air fatality
In only 30 days

June Third
1539
Hernando DeSoto claimed Florida for Spain
The queen would be content
It seemed a good idea at the time
But we all know how that went

> **Plants answer phones by saying "Aloe"**

June Fourth
1984
Bruce Springsteen was on top
Of the world this very day
When he released his album
"Born in the U.S.A."

June Fifth
1783
The Montgolfier brothers
Found the time opportune
For being the first
To fly in a balloon

June Sixth
1641
Spain lost Portugal
No one could believe it
So the King asked the army
"Where did you last leave it?"

> *Silly Putty was invented by accident in 1943 as a substitute for rubber*

> **On the Titanic, all hull broke loose**

June Seventh
1769
Daniel Boone
An adventurer plucky
Begins exploring
The territory of Kentucky

June Eighth
1869
Ives McGaffey
With irony did construct
The first vacuum cleaner
It really truly sucked

June Ninth
1967
Hey, hey you know they
Were on a big roll
When the Monkees appeared
At the Hollywood Bowl

June Tenth
1752
Benjamin Franklin
Spent the night
Teasing the lightning
With his kite

> **Farmers have detractors. They also have deplows**

June Eleventh
1982
No reversed charges
On his galactic phone
It was revealed today
When E.T. first dialed home

> *Mark Twain's birth and death coincide with Halley's Comet*

The Odd Farmer's Almanac for 2021

The greatest scientist was a Pauling

June Twelfth
1931
When it came to corruption
Al Capone had large amounts
In recognition of it
Indictments on 5000 counts

June Thirteenth
1854
Anthony Faas
With no instrument to play
Went out and patented
The accordion today

June Fourteenth
1922
President Warren Harding
Took a bit to be convinced
To be the first prez on radio
They've been talking ever since

June Fifteenth
1911
Tabulating Computing Recording Corp.
Was incorporated back then
But you may know them better now
As the company IBM

An eclipse is a difficult phase the moon is going through

June Sixteenth
1961
Rudolph Nureyev was gone before
His absence got detected
In Paris on this very day
The ballet star defected

June Seventeenth
1579
Sir Francis Drake exploring
Declared upon this day
He claimed for Queen and country
San Francisco Bay

Sean Connery made millions in the Bond market

June Eighteenth
1994
O.J. Simpson, facing charges
Saw prospects all nose dive
So he took his Bronco through LA
On a lovely afternoon drive

June Nineteenth
1963
Valentina Tereshkova
Really knew her place
Becoming the first woman
To go to outer space

June Twentieth
1837
Victoria really
Broke the mold
Becoming queen
At 18 years old

June Twenty First
1529
Queen Catherine of England
After a big stunt was pulled
Tried to get her marriage
To Henry unannulled

June Twenty Second
1868
After their secession
Met with no success
The Confederate state of Arkansas
Came back to the U.S.

Television was invented only two years after the invention of sliced bread

"Diplomacy is the art of saying 'Nice doggie' until you can find a rock" - Will Rogers

The Odd Farmer's Almanac for 2021

Nostrildamus - a seer who predicts plastic surgery results

Hot pants are thermal outerwear

June Twenty Third
1960
It would change the world
For Jack's girlfriend Jill
When the U.S. began selling
The birth control pill

June Twenty Fourth
1916
Because of the fans
That she would attract
Mary Pickford's the first actress
With a million dollar contract

June Twenty Fifth
1951
The prettiest thing
You ever did see
The very first broadcast
Of color TV

June Twenty Eighth
1935
Not a good idea keeping
Our gold in a box
So FDR mandated
A vault at Fort Knox

June Twenty Ninth
1964
The Civil Rights Act
Finally passes muster
After an 83 day
Filibuster

June Thirtieth
1908
The Tunguska fireball
A Siberian mystery
The greatest meteor explosion
In recorded history

The Frisbee was originally released in 1957 as the "Pluto Platter"

Gilda Radner born 6/28/1946

Divorce is the high cost of loving

June Twenty Sixth
1963
JFK In West Berlin
Trying to out-reach
Said "I'm a jelly donut"
In a famous speech

June Twenty Seventh
1955
In Illinois
The public saw
The very first
Seat belt law

Opus the Penguin was "born" 6/26/81

To Be or Not?

I had self doubts, late yesterday
A crisis existential
Am I for real or might I be
A dream inconsequential?

Descartes said, "I think, therefore I am"
To prove his own existence
Because to be, there must be something
Making that insistence

Just like Descartes, I thought a lot
So I had to be, wahoo!
But in view of that, I must confess
I'm not so sure of you

The Odd Farmer's Almanac for 2021

Famous People Party

A party invitation just was
Sent to famous greats
A lot of them are coming
The news we all await

Newton said that he'd drop in
But **Pavlov** simply drooled
Ohm resisted heartily
While **Kelvin** went and cooled

Samuel Morse dashed off a note
Expressing just one thought
He'd be there very timely, yes
In fact, right on the dot

Darwin said he'd be there if
His schedule got resolved
Until that happens, he will wait
And see how things evolve

Volta said he wouldn't come
But I think that he lied
Because I heard that parties leave him
Quite electrified

Edison's acting negative
About it, what a schlup!
If he comes to the party
I hope he lightens up

Einstein wrote back quickly with
An answer short and cheesy
He said for him attendance would
Be relatively easy

The Invisible Man will not be there
His response was rather numbing
He snottily declared no way
That he could see himself coming

Famous People Party

Dr. Jekyll said the time
Is bad for him that date
And also, he really hasn't felt
Much like himself of late

Heisenberg is uncertain if
He has the time to spare
And **Hamlet** wasn't clear if he
Would be or not be there

James Watt declared the party'd be
Like something in a dream
And he's been looking for a way
To just left off some steam

A message now has come that says
The brothers known as **Wright**
Will be there if the two of them
Can find themselves a flight

Vince Van Gogh will not be there
There's no way he'll commit
In fact, when asked if he would come
He wouldn't 'ear of it

Audubon has commitments then
But hopes that he can swing it
Until then, it's up in the air
Perhaps he'll have to wing it

Gene Roddenberry's far away,
But wrote back, "What the heck?"
"I'll do whatever I can do"
"To undertake the Trek"

Jonas Salk will try his best
He'd like to come a lot
He'll plan his schedule carefully
To give it the best shot

Harry and Meghan's Departure was a Reign Drain

The Odd Farmer's Almanac for 2021

Famous People Party

I hope that **Calvin Klein** will come
Oh wouldn't that be great?
But knowing him, I'm sure he'll be
Quite fashionably late

Henry the Eighth will be there and
Deep down inside, I knew it
Because he told his friends that he
Would soon be heading to it

Tarzan said he's busy
He'll give it the college try
And if his schedule lets him
He's happy to swing by

Eli Whitney's gonna come
And that's a big win-win
Because he'll bring refreshments
Most likely 'twill be gin

Schrodinger cannot decide
His plans I do not know
Confusingly he told me that
He may and may not go

Steinway RSVPed to say
That he would really love it
To help remember, he said that he
Would make a note of it

The **Maytag Repairman's** almost sure
Unless there's a fly in the ointment
That likely won't be a problem cuz
He never has appointments

Jesse James was iffy
In the long note that he penned
He said if he's held up somewhere
He definitely won't attend

Famous People Party

Ishmael's excited
Expects it to be sublime
He's really looking forward to
A whale of a good time

Amelia Earhart won't be there
The problem's not the cost
Each time she goes somewhere
She ends up getting lost

Copernicus would enjoy it
But the chances are rather slim
He's not the best of guests because
The world revolves around him

I'm afraid **Godot** may not be here
Upon this happy occasion
The last I heard from him, he said
He was waiting on the invitation

The thought that **Niels** will be there
Is enough to make me snore
The issue's when I talk to him
He really is a **Bohr**

And **Madame Curie** will attend
I'm sure she'll look quite clever
She'll probably be like always
As radiant as ever

Helen Keller isn't sure
She'd like to very much
And when she has an answer
She said she'd be in touch

Stephen Hawking responded
To say as we begin
We'll see him once again that day
When he comes rolling in

The flat-Earther traveler eventually came around

Famous People Party

Ms Antoinette's conditional
It's weird, for goodness sake
She says that she will be there
But only if there's cake

Coulomb had a question
For him it loomed quite large
He needs to know before he comes
If there will be a charge

Mickey Mouse's refusal
Has left me rather numb
He says he's feeling goofy
And so he cannot come

Geiger's all excited
The prospect has him humming
He wrote to tell me that I should
Count on him a coming

Tiger Woods sends his regrets
That he cannot arrive
The problem was he said it was
Too far for him to drive

Hamlet had a question
He directed back at me
Asking if the address was
2B or not 2B

Beethoven too was iffy
He needs to know some more
He said it's only possible
If he is able to score

Ferris Bueller's affirmative
For enjoying party quaff
He said no prob in coming
Because it's his day off

Famous People Party

Lincoln said he might be late
His travel causes stress
He's coming in from Gettysburg
And needs the right address

And **Noah's** another iffy one
His secretary explains
She says he'll come if it is nice
But not with heavy rains

And last, not least, **Tom Brady** said
He'd not be there, alas
He's prepping for the season and
Will simply have to pass

Adding Up

Some say the age of 60 is
What used to be just 40
A time for folks to still be running
Around in something sporty

Perhaps that's true, but I don't think
The observation's right
Cuz for me at 60 years of age
10:00 pm is the new midnight

"It would be nice to spend billions on schools and roads, but right now that money is desperately needed for political ads."
– Andy Borowitz

"The best thing about the future is that it comes one day at a time."
– Abraham Lincoln

The Odd Farmer's Almanac for 2021

It's a Beautiful Day For a Bark

It's a beautiful day for a bark
Perhaps we could go to the park
No sittin' and stayin'
I'd rather be playin'
It's a beautiful day for a bark

It's a wonderful life as a mutt
When folks look at me and say "What"
"Is your pedigree?"
Doesn't matter, I'm me
It's a wonderful life as a mutt

It's incredible being a cur
With fleas underneath all my fur
If they gave me the manual
I would not be a spaniel
It's incredible being a cur

Could we go take a walk in the park?
I would sure like to run, jump and bark
You could throw me a stick
I could learn a new trick
If we could just go to the park

A dog really is our best friend
Beside us right up til the end
Squeezing seven years of fun
In each trip around the sun
A dog really is our best friend

Chefs are panhandlers

No-Brainer
The zombie apocalypse is coming
'Twill be the next big wave
They're seeking out good brains to eat
Relax, my friend, you're safe

When the Covid Thing is Over

When the Covid thing is over
Some things I'm gonna do
Like walking down a sidewalk
Without avoiding you

No masks to clean for "just in case"
I'll have a party at my place
My hands will touch and rub my face
I'll hug a friend or two

No social distance rules to keep
No frets of spray in every peep
No nightmares when I go to sleep
Perhaps a barbecue

We'll hike with friends for many miles
No curves to flatten and meanwhile
We'll get back to our old lifestyle
These things are just a few

Yes, I'll rejoice, no more indoors
Plus no more bad infection scores
And toilet paper in the stores
Hang on and we'll pull through

Science is Golden
COVID, measles
Polio, cancer
No matter the question
Science is the answer

Silence is Golden
If you've nothing smart to say
Here's my advice, please try it
One way you never will be wrong
Is simply keeping quiet

Balloons hate pop music

Page 57

Career Considerations

Employment in the world today
Is causing much unease
Let's take a look at how it would
Affect these specialties

When McDonalds owners lose the place
That each of them has prized
Do they find out that they've become
Simply **disenfranchised**?

Dry cleaners work each day quite hard
To keep us nicely dressed
But if customers do not come in
Are they suddenly **depressed**?

Reporters writing stories may
Sometimes create a mess
If the editor calls them out on it
Are they totally **depressed**?

Those fisherman out fishing for
The fish they have awaited
May not be fishing very long
If they have been **debated**

A mattress seller's troubles start
When products are defunct
And if that should occur to them
Do they just get **debunked**?

All brides are lovely ladies
Their partners can't resist
But in the act of marrying
Should we say they are **dismissed**?

The organ donor thinking of
The operation shivered
For when it all was over
He knew he'd be delivered

And what about that movie star
The director just now blamed?
If he cuts her from the starring role
Will she then be **defamed**?

Cuteness is
a brush with the awww

Career Considerations

The castles too do not escape
Admonishment, it's noted
But when it happens to them
Do they just get **demoated**?

And what about hair stylists
When problems get addressed?
Would it be fair to ask if they
Are suddenly **distressed**?

A sailor who has gone AWOL
May find out he's been thwarted
If he's dismissed, will the record say
That he was just **deported**?

The pastry chef's in trouble
His boss has been alerted
There's troubles in the kitchen
For this, is he **desserted**?

The teacher working in the class
Is feeling rather jaded
Because the principal stated that
She now has been **downgraded**

And then there are the strippers
When their stripping is concluded
If they did not work out will they
Find out they've been **denuded**?

And last, about podiatrists
If work goes uncompleted
Will the boss who lets them go declare
That they have been **defeeted**?

"A woman is like a tea bag – you can't tell how strong she is until you put her in hot water."
– Eleanor Roosevelt

"Leave something for someone but don't leave someone for something."
– Enid Blyton

The Odd Farmer's Almanac for 2021

JULY 2021

July is the height of summer fun and the time patriotic Americans celebrate and proudly display their independence by launching "bombs bursting in air" and firecrackers that are mostly, um, uh, made in China. More specifically, most of the U.S. fireworks are made in Hunan Province in China and if that rings a bell, it's because your brain wasn't damaged by the virus that erupted from that same province last year and caused a bit of mayhem (some described it as a pandemic) around the world. You may have heard about it.

If you actually want to buy fireworks made in the U.S., you'll have a hard time finding them. Fortunately, there is another option for fireworks that are truly "Made in the USA" and it's surprisingly simple - make your own. Believe it or not, it's not that hard and it doesn't require any fancy equipment at all. Here's how to do it and save some money. After a long hard day at work, announce to your spouse that you miss last year's Covid-based quarantine and have decided this year to take another "staycation" with the family to save money and get to know each other even better. That's all there is to it! The "rockets' red glare" won't compare with the reaction you're gonna to get. BOOM! Be careful, though. Homemade fireworks can be unpredictable due to very short fuses. Also, remember to work outdoors in the event of unexpected explosions.

With summer, of course, comes heat and (in most of the U.S.) humidity. Where I grew up in the Midwest, the thermometer often exceeded 100° F accompanied by soul-melting humidity. Everyone was miserable, but the one thing that eased the discomfort for kids and made us happy was a Popsicle®. Moms promised a Popsicle as a way of encouraging good behavior and it worked, most of the time. Popsicles, which were originally named "Epsicle Ice Pops" after their creator, Frank Epperson, came into being in 1905

> Popsicles weren't actually invented as much as they were discovered. Mr. Epperson had been experimenting with making a powdered flavoring for soft drinks when one night he left his product along with a stirring stick in a container on his back porch. When he arose in the morning, the freezing temperatures overnight had frozen the stick in the sweet concoction, creating the first Popsicle.

The race of text towards the bottom of this page reminds me, as always, that it is time for the July astronomical forecast. By now, you could probably do most of this yourself, but since it is my job, I'll lay it out once again. The moon continues with its every cyclic ways that include half (July 1), new (July 9), half (July 17), full (July 23), and half again (July 31). Venus and Mercury tango on July 13, as do the moon and Mercury (July 7), the moon with both Mars and Mercury on the 12th, the moon and Saturn (July 24) and the moon and Jupiter (July 25). The Earth also reaches its farthest point from the sun on July 5. And if that isn't enough, there are two meteor showers to enjoy - the Piscis Austranids on the 28th and the alpha-Capricornids on the 30th. You've been good while reading this, so go have a Popsicle.

The Odd Farmer's Almanac for 2021

> **Old colanders never die. They just can't handle the strain**

> **McDonald's new T-bone dinner is a big McSteak**

July First
1963
Reflecting that
The U.S. growed
The Postal Service
Started Zip Code

July Second
1937
Even today
We find it weird
That Amelia Earhart
Disappeared

July Third
1890
Idaho really
Is feeling great
Admitted as
The 43rd state

July Fourth
1895
"America the Beautiful"
Describes a great view
And on this day made
Its printed debut

July Fifth
1942
His James Bond books
Would later tantalize
Ian Fleming graduates
From a training school for spies

July Sixth
1957
This is the day
That started it all
When a Beatle called John
Met a guy named Paul

July Seventh
1928
The craziest thing
Anyone had seen
Bread that was sliced
By a machine

July Eighth
1913
Alfred Carlton Gilbert
A name you won't forget
Received a patent on this day
For his Erector Set

July Ninth
1956
Known as the eternal teenager
Dick Clark knew the bands
He started on this very day
Hosting American Bandstand

July Tenth
1040
Raising awareness of high taxes
Something everybody knows
Lady Godiva rode on horseback
Devoid of all her clothes

July Eleventh
1804
The most famous U.S. duel
That ever would occur
Took place when Mister Hamilton
Was killed by Aaron Burr

"Airplane!" released 7/2/1980

Dave Barry born 7/3/1947

"An economist's guess is liable to be as good as anybody else's" – Will Rogers

> For transplant surgery I did go
> To fix the foot I hurt, you know
> The donor for it didn't show
> They used some candy, big uh-oh
> Now I have a Tic-Tac Toe

Page 60

The Odd Farmer's Almanac for 2021

> **Sixty is the new forty, but there's a big difference. Twenty.**

July Twelfth
1957
Surgeon General Burney
Came forward with an answer
Declaring to all that smoking
Is a leading cause of lung cancer

July Thirteenth
1865
Horace Greeley
Had a plan
Declaring to all
"Go west, young man"

July Fourteenth
1938
Howard Hughes
Working day and night
Set a new record
For around the world flight

July Fifteenth
1898
The Italian Camilio Golgi
Examining cells quite thin
Discovered the cell apparatus
That was named for him

July Sixteenth
1951
He was a recluse
We don't know why
J.D. Salinger
Published "Catcher in the Rye"

> "Always go to other people's funerals, otherwise they won't come to yours" - Yogi Berra

July Seventeenth
1070
Perhaps it was because
Of all the name's slanders
That Arnulf the Hapless
Became the Earl of Flanders

July Eighteenth
1938
"Wrong Way" Corrigan was going to California
But did not know which way to head
And then 28 hours later
He landed in Ireland instead

July Nineteenth
1799
The key to hieroglyphics
Was found in a village today
The Rosetta stone made possible
What we know of old language today

> The hacker criminal went data way

> **Makeup artists give Powder to the People**

What I Write

I like to write my verses
I like to sing my songs
They both to me are curses
I often do them wrong

My meter's weak, my voice is worse
It is a very special curse

But gee
I think you would agree
I'm not at all a victim
Instead that label falls upon
Those on whom I inflict 'em

> **Ancient Trojans were a condom nation**

The Odd Farmer's Almanac for 2021

> **Stubborn old people go to resisted living**

July Twentieth
1969
Neil and Buzz walk swiftly
On a sunny afternoon
When they were done they left behind
Their footprints on the moon

July Twenty First
1865
It simply wasn't big enough
For two of them in one town
So Wild Bill Hickok killed Davis Tutt
In the first wild west showdown

July Twenty Second
1967
Jimi Hendrix did his thing
But everyone agrees
He did it right by quitting from
Opening for the Monkees

July Twenty Third
1904
An amazing man
Who changed the game
Jackie Robinson inducted
Into the Hall of Fame

July Twenty Fourth
1917
On trial as a spy
Refusing to say sorry
The Dutch exotic dancer
Known as Mata Hari

July Twenty Fifth
1999
The first of seven in a row
But it was oh so wrong
It was, of course, the steroid use
By cyclist Lance Armstrong

Neal Gladstone's Birthday, July 23

"I'm such a good lover because I practice a lot on my own" - Woody Allen

July Twenty Sixth
1775
Benjamin Franklin
Became on this day
First Postmaster General
Of the USA

July Twenty Seventh
1586
Dear Sir Walter Raleigh
They should have told you 'no'
When you brought to England
The very first tobacco

July Twenty Eighth
1933
Rudy Vallee
Quite the man
Received the first
Singing telegram

July Twenty Ninth
1927
If you had to have it
Its praises you sung
Today was the very first
Installed iron lung

July Thirtieth
2017
Computer hackers
In the know
Stole Games of Thrones
From HBO

July Thirty First
1922
Ralph Samuelson glided
On the water to be
The very first person
To water ski

"I looked up my family tree and found out I was the sap" - Rodney Dangerfield

> **Picky people are trite and true**

Page 62

The Odd Farmer's Almanac for 2021

The Summer We Made Michael Invisible

I grew up in the tiny farm town of Fowler, Illinois, which, on a big day, had a population of 200 people and just about as many dogs and cats. I had asthma very bad as a kid and was allergic to ragweed, hay, and virtually everything found in the farm air surrounding our town. Most of my friends lived on farms and others worked on farms, which was something I couldn't do with my allergies. Idleness left me plenty of time for what John Lennon called "Mind Games" and I put it to good use, doing what my wife now calls "living inside my head."

There was a family down the street from us with kids a few years younger than me - closer to my brother's age. Stanley and Michael were good friends of my brother Brian and me. I was the oldest of the pack by about six years so I, as they say, should have been a better example than I was in this story.

Summer was the most boring time of year and boredom is one of the worst things for teenage boys, at least as far as keeping out of mischief. I couldn't work, didn't have others my age in town, and was too young to drive, so that left me with all kinds of chances to think, develop my imagination and use it mostly for my own amusement.

One source of mischief, or as I like to think of it, youthful creativity, involved outhouses - outdoor toilets. Outhouses are the absolute funniest things in the world - at least to the 14 year-old I was at the time. Typically about 5 feet square at the base and tall enough to stand up in, many were what we called two seaters because they allowed two people to relieve themselves side-by-side. While the thought seems a bit revolting, it had a practical purpose in the midst of a frigid Illinois winter when nature calls, because two bodies gave off more heat than one. I still get the shivers thinking about it. And don't get me started about splinters.

When I was growing up in the 1950s and 60s in Fowler, about 20% of the people in town used outdoor toilets, since their houses did not have indoor plumbing. We had an indoor toilet, but the people on either side of us did not. Our house sat on a hill at the base of which was the house of Goldie Robbins and she was the object of some of my mind games.

Now, despite what it may sound like in what follows, I liked Goldie, got along with her well, and I think she liked me, but I found her comical in her short, stubby appearance and her extremely animated, furious reactions when riled. Goldie always seemed like a balloon ready to pop. A time-tested way to light Goldie's fuse involved her outhouse and the walnuts that fell from two giant trees on the side of our house.

With nothing else to do on a long, hot day, we would wait for Goldie to make the inevitable long stroll from her house to go reconnect with nature in her backyard privy. Goldie was very noisy, very slow and very patterned, so it was easy to know what she was up to. It typically started with her yelling back into the house to one of her sons or her husband to do this or that as she left the house. At that point, the screen door, which was on a tight spring, would slam shut behind her.

Following a short trudge to the outdoor plumbing structure and a lock of its door, we'd spring into action, assuming strategic positions behind sheds, trees, and bushes in our yard so as not to be seen. Armed with walnuts, we would wait for evidence

The Summer We Made Michael Invisible

that "action" was taking place and then we'd start flinging our bombs at the roof of the tiny box in which Goldie sat. This would generate a rustling noise from inside and she'd come scrambling out shouting at whoever it was that was doing this AGAIN, but since we were hidden, she was shouting at the air.

This went on, over and over - the same pattern. Creaking noise of the front door, Goldie hollering into the house, slamming of the screen door, trudging to the outhouse, walnut bombardment, Goldie screaming at the sky, no one to be seen. Over and over. No matter how many times we did it, it was always hilarious to us. Now, let me say, I'm not proud of what we did and I blame it on youthful exuberance/indiscretion, but what was done is history and it WAS funny. We did get caught one time and that story takes a bit more telling.

It involved the youngest of the four of us, the neighbor boy named Michael. Michael was the most inclined to believe what older kids, such as the three of us, who should have known better, told him. We were always filling Michael with crazy stories and, being the trusting, gentle soul that he was, he accepted them at face value. Yes, it was a form of bullying that I deplore today, but those were unenlightened times and I was certainly a clueless young man. I will say in a mild defense that we never intended harm. The same was true of our actions toward Goldie. While there were some in the town who would push over or "tip" an outhouse, thus destroying it, that was wrong to me because it was mean and destructive and all I was interested in was fun.

One hot, humid Illinois summer afternoon, I got the bright idea we should convince Michael he was invisible. This involved a magic wand in the form of a stick, a few contrived abracadabra-like words, and the other three of us pretending that he had disappeared. Well, it worked, in spades, unfortunately for Michael and the rest of us, as it turned out. Michael really "liked" being invisible. He told us how he was able to fly and float above the clouds. Michael clearly had his own mind games and being invisible helped inspire them. It was great fun and seemed harmless at the time. He would often ask us to make him invisible and we gladly complied. This went on for the better part of a summer.

Well - you can probably see this coming - during one of Michael's invisible episodes, Goldie made her afternoon trek and, as usual, we assumed our strategic positions. All, except Michael, that is, who didn't feel the need to hide because, after all, he was invisible. When you've got a superpower, it's a waste not to use it, right?

Emboldened by faux transparency, Michael grabbed a handful of walnuts, marched straight to Goldie's outhouse and, with her seated inside, proceeded to pelt it. Like clockwork, Goldie raced out screaming and, for the first time, saw the perpetrator - the very visible Michael, who was smiling his face off. She screamed at him about how she was going to tell his mother and he was going to get in SO much trouble for what he was doing. In response, Michael did something none of us ever thought we'd see - he yelled back at her, "You can't see me, I'm invisible." As long as I live, I'll never forget that scene. Well, needless to say, things went downhill from there.

The Odd Farmer's Almanac for 2021

The Summer We Made Michael Invisible

Yes, it was hilarious. Yes, Goldie cocked her head upon learning of Michael's invisibility. Yes, Goldie called Michael's mother. Yes, all of us got in trouble, and deservedly so. Yes, we never made Michael invisible again. And yes, I still laugh thinking about it. Goldie passed away before I ever atoned for disrupting her bowel movements, but I did make one attempt. I wrote a song/video inspired by her son who died of lung cancer. It's on YouTube at https://www.youtube.com/watch?v=scG1mqupjPw

Welcome to Microshaft Word

Welcome to Microshaft Word 21.0, the most advanced word processing system in the world. Please begin typing and our content wizard will help you to format your document.

Dear Sir:

This appears to be a letter. Would you like Microshaft Word to format this document as a letter?
Please select an option: YES / NO

YES

Dear Sir:

YES.

You appear to be attempting to delete the word 'YES from your letter that begins "Dear Sir:". Would you like Microshaft Word to delete the word 'YES for you?
Please select an option: YES / NO

YES

Dear ir:

Warning: Due to an unexpected internal error, Micro haft Word i now unable to di play the letter ' '.

Indoor plumbing gave Napolean his water loo

Would you prefer to ub titute another letter in it place?
Plea e elect an option: YE /NO

YE

Which letter would you like Micro haft Word to
ub titute in it place?

&

The character you have cho en, "&" i not an acceptable ub titute letter. Plea e choo e one of the character from the following li t:

a / b / c / d / e / f / g / h / i / j / k / l / m /
n / o / p / r / / t / u / v / w / x / y / z

j

You have picked the letter 'j'. Microjhaft Word will jubjtitute the letter 'j' for the letter ' '.

Dear Jir:

The word you have entered, "Jir", ij not in the Microjhaft Word dictionary. What would you like to do?

Welcome to Microshaft Word

Pleaje jelect an option: ADD 'Jir' to Dictionary / JUGGEJT jpelling / IGNORE

JUGGEJT jpelling

I cannot underjtand what you mean by the phraje "JUGGEJT jpelling". Pleaje enter again
Pleaje jelect an option: ADD 'Jir' to Dictionary / JUGGEJT jpelling / IGNORE

You have ujed the mouje to jelect the option 'JUGGEJT jpelling'. Pleaje jelect a word from the following lijt to replace "Jir":

Jig / Jar / Jim / Jif / Mir / Air / Jir /

You have ujed the mouje to jelect the word "Jir" to replace the word "Jir".

Dear Jir:

The word, "Jir" you have entered appearj to be a name. Would you like Microjhaft Word to look in your addrejj book for Jir'j addrejj? Pleaje jelect an option: YEJ / NO

Go to hell

Rejponje 'Go' accepted aj 'No'.

Dear Jir:

to hell

The phraje "to hell" that you have entered ij not punctuated properly for jtarting a jentence. In addition, you appear to be attempting to delete the phraje from your letter to Jir. Would you like Microjhaft

Socrates didn't do so well with the Hemlock Maneuver

Word to delete the phraje "to hell" or did you mean to type 'HELP' injtead of 'hell'?

Pleaje jelect an option: DELETE 'to hell' / HELP

HELP

Welcome to the Microjoft Word HELP Jyjtem. To get HELP on a topic enter a phraje dejcribing what you want to do:

Jcrew Microjhaft

I'm jorry, I don't underjtand the phraje " Jcrew MicroJhaft". Pleaje check your jpelling and enter again.

...

You appear to be attempting to jhut down without javing your letter to Ji . . . . . .

July Thoughts

The month did surely go by fast
As everyone "vacated"
The town feels empty, now at last
For summer we've awaited

But peace is lost with auto noise
From mufflers loud and grating
Some say they're toys for little boys
Just overcompensating

But you will not hear me attack
These autos I've deplored
Cuz I know that a pen, in fact
Is mightier than a Ford

Before I go, vacation's here
Goodbye to winter's glooms
And when your motor home's in gear
You're driving three bed-varooms

Word Play

The injury I had at work
Is causing me to strain
That is to be expected when
You're having LABOR PAINS

A man who studied paintings
Knew the right place to be
Examining all the work down at
The local ARTERY

The cafeteria's exit door
Is in the rear right near ya
Or as they tell the customers
"It's there in the BACTERIA"

The sight of blood caused me to faint
It was an awful scare
I was in my doctor's office and
Now I'm an OUTPATIENT there

Long ago in ancient Rome
When they had a big election
One voting zone was quite well known
It was the CAESARIAN SECTION

A little lie, that's all it was
Not deceitful, proud, or bold
I didn't think it mattered much
That FIBULA I told

My plumbing sprung a leak just now
I think I'm in dire straits
It's after five and the plumbers say
They're going to charge NITRATES

And finally, I havea cold
The medicine costs many bucks
I caught it at the airport and
This TERMINAL ILLNESS sucks

Once

In school as just a youngster
My teacher - rather gruff
She gave me much anxiety
Once was more than enough

I remember crying badly
Being told I should be tough
Stereotypical male upbringing
Once was more than enough

And then there was that acne
My face got oh so rough
That teenage angst, uncertainty
Once was more than enough

In the 70s there was streaking
Running around in the buff
What in the hell were we thinking?
Once was more than enough

I came of age, I hit my stride
I felt I was hot stuff
And when I learned rejection
Once was more than enough

So now I'm getting older
Retirement and all that stuff
Despite all my misgivings
Once is not enough

Modern Soldiers

In viral times
With troubling norms
Soldiers wear
Different uniforms

(Support Essential Workers)

AUGUST 2021

Besides being mostly hot and a popular vacation month, August isn't really known for much. The end of vacay time is on its horizon, which means the start of the school year is approaching, an event typically viewed oppositely by parents and their children. In the West, it's a time of wildfires, events viewed oppositely by seasonal firefighters and homeowners. Christmas is also inching ever closer, an event viewed oppositely by advertisers and the rest of the world - only 116 shopping days til Xmas at the start the month.

So August is really hot and dull with a lot of opposites and come to think of it, 'hot' and 'dull' are opposites as well, if we're talking about bedtime clothing, sex symbols, and inspirational speakers, but not knives, solar power, or jalapeño peppers and don't even think about stolen property. You're thinking about stolen property now, aren't you?

The month of August does have the best meteor shower of the year, so perhaps we should talk about the astronomical forecast here, since the month isn't exactly helping us out in the interesting feature department. The moon, which is neither hot, nor dull (at least if you're in love), cycles through its phases of new, half, full, and half on the days of August 8, 15, 22, and 30, respectively. The moon does the opposite of social distancing during the month with Mars (9th), Venus (10-11), Saturn, (20th), and Jupiter (21-22). Mercury and Mars do their thing on the 18th. That meteor shower of interest is the Perseids and it occurs on the 12th. The best time to see the Perseids is after midnight. The waxing moon will bring a fair amount of light to the sky, which makes for poorer viewing, unfortunately. And last, although it technically isn't astronomical, the amount of press it got was - August 24 is officially known as "Pluto Got Demoted Day."

Besides being a month, august (written lowercase) is an adjective, meaning respected and impressive. One could, for example say that "August was august" or "August was August" and have two different meanings. You could also say "It was an august August." And if you were speaking to someone named August, you could say "It was an august August, August". If it was a windy month, you might say to your friend named August, "It was an august, August, August. A gust of wind blew all month." If you were surprised by said wind, you might say, "It was an august August, August. Aghast, a gust of wind blew all month."

And, speaking of first names, August was the actual first name of the person more commonly called "Anheuser Busch." He, of course, is the person who built one of several U.S.-based empires dedicated to serving beer drinkers who not only want a beer that is "Less Filling," but also "Tastes Meh.". August Anheuser Busch also owned the St. Louis Cardinals. His name and the baseball connection may bring to mind the term "Bush League," but there is, as they say in the reporting biz, no relation.

As we close the door on this, the hardest of all months to write something funny about, let us not forget August is national breastfeeding month, national eye exam month, and national immunization awareness month. I collapse in a creative heap.

The Odd Farmer's Almanac for 2021

August First
1498
Columbus, we know
Didn't even get close
Missed India again
At the Venezuelan coast

August Second
1610
Henry Hudson
On this day
Went and discovered
His own bay

> **The new bug spray for dolphins "Flipper Off"**

August Third
1936
Racing before Hitler
Jesse Owens was bold
Winning the first
Of his four medals gold

August Fourth
1855
A wonderful payoff
After years of notation
John Bartlett published
"Familiar Quotations"

August Fifth
1884
To welcome tired, poor and hungry
Into their new home
The Statue of Liberty
Got its cornerstone

August Sixth
1926
In the English Channel
With confidence brimming
Gertrude Ederle made it
The first woman swimming

> **30 days of ice cream make a month of sundaes**

"I don't think anyone should write their autobiography until after they're dead" - Samuel Goldwyn

August Seventh
1961
Nikita Kruschev
Had the nerve to suggest
That their economy
Would pass the U.S.

August Eighth
1974
After his duties
Had been forsaken
Nixon resigned
For the Watergate break-in

August Ninth
1859
Though one wouldn't be built
Till many years later
A patent was issued
For the first escalator

> **ESPN is all about game airage**

August Tenth
1889
Dan Rylands tired
Of bottle mishaps
Inventing the first
Screw top cap

August Eleventh
1964
A zillion teenagers
Screamed and cheered
When "A Hard Day's Night"
In New York premiered

> **Misspellers have Guardian Angles**

Editors have rewording careers

The Odd Farmer's Almanac for 2021

> It rains so much in Oregon, Xmas bell ringers work for the Salvation Navy

August Twelfth
1930
Clarence Birdseye
A real chilling dude
Got a patent for inventing
Quick freezing food

August Thirteenth
1889
Though today it may seem
Rather quaint and quite funny
A phone patent permitted
Calls using money

August Fourteenth
1846
Thoreau took his protest
Up to the max
And got jailed for refusing
To pay up his tax

August Fifteenth
1937
The Appalachian trail
An unbroken chain
2000 miles
From Georgia to Maine

August Sixteenth
1896
Interest in the far north
Certainly spiked
With discovery of gold
In the Klondike

Kung Flu infects martial artists

Steve Martin born 8/15/1945

August Seventeenth
1903
Joe Pulitzer
With journalistic ties
Donates a million bucks
To start the Pulitzer prize

August Eighteenth
1909
The mayor of Tokyo
Liking what he sees
Gives Washington, DC
2000 cherry trees

August Nineteenth
2008
Critics mostly
Were very pleased
When Lady Gaga's first album
Got released

August Twentieth
1882
In Moscow, a symphony
Majestic for sure
Tchaikosky's
1812 Overture

August Twenty First
1858
Who knew the drama
These two would create?
The first of several
Lincoln-Douglas debates

August Twenty Second
1902
Thinking it might
Help him to go far
Teddy Roosevelt became
The first Prez in a car

Ogden Nash born - 8/19/1902

Dorothy Parker born 8/22/1893

> The assemble it yourself Apple car is called iKia

> My rabbit stew has a hare in it

Page 70

The Odd Farmer's Almanac for 2021

August Twenty Third
1962
A way for broadcasts
To travel far
Europe and American
Celebrate Telstar

August Twenty Fourth
1853
Now eaten at
A furious clip
Mr. George Crum
Invents potato chips

August Twenty Fifth
1609
Glowing with pride
Over his creation
Galileo performed
His telescope demonstration

August Twenty Sixth
1947
Don Bankhead has
Two great baseball stats
The first black pitcher
And a homer in his first at bat

August Twenty Seventh
2008
Today there was
A political precedent
First African American
Nominated for President

> A Chinese lady bought Indian clothing. It's Hu's sari now.

August Twenty Eighth
1845
Today it's still
A big success
Scientific American
Rolled off the press

> "An apple a day keeps anyone away, if you throw it hard enough" - Anonymous

> At the fork in the road - no parking, any tine

August Twenty Ninth
1896
Not where you'd
Expect it to be
Chop Suey invented
In NYC

August Thirtieth
1972
A really amazing
Flipping nut
The gold goes to
Olga Korbut

August Thirty First
1925
With her Samoan studies
On coming of age
Margaret Meade truly
Was all the rage

> The politician was so fat, he could only walk for office

> Bar-B-Cue pork is good at picnics

Haute Date

Last night I had
A real hot date
And I was
Feeling great

Unfortunately
My date was late
Because of this
I gained some wait

August Meditations

Oh summer, how the time we savored
Such great fun with you
A brief release for good behavior
But ending, now it's true

Motor homers packed all day
Crammed their vans, then drove away
These people really have odd zen
Getting away from it all
Means taking it with them

It isn't just for long vacations
That toys get brought along
Because right now in education
Technology sings its song

Papers, pencils, notebooks, rulers
Things once packaged up for schoolers
Now iPhones, Web and internet
Are what it seems each child must get

When school begins, this coming autumn
Modern parents will have bought 'em
And modern teachers too will find
That no iPad gets left behind

So thank you teachers, every one
I truly have been blessed
Although it wasn't always fun
I really can attest
That verses writ by fools like me
Began with learning ABCs

> "I can't understand why a person will take a year to write a novel when he can easily buy one for a few dollars."
> – Fred Allen

Albuquerque University Promotional Flyer

At Albuquerque University, we're committed to providing online degrees to meet the complex interdisciplinary challenges of today's world. Towards that end, we offer courses in almost every aspect of academic endeavor. Check out our offerings below.

Theological Ecology
TE 251: Texas Oil Derrick Massacres
Turning away from traditional views of habitat preservation, TE 251 examines the Alaskan National Wildlife Arctic Reserve and other environmentally sensitive areas employing the biblical imperative, "Where would Jesus drill?" Register for TE 251 and help determine if a divine divining rod can find ecologically safe oil where others have failed. Prerequisite - TE 250 ("Oil in the Family").

Molecular and Musical Biology
MMB 371: Avian Flu Is for Losers
What if the Recording Industry Association of America (RIAA) tried to stop the spread of HIV, West Nile, and other viruses instead of MP3s? Could replication of these deadly killers somehow be slowed while at the same time freeing music lovers to download songs on demand without cost or penalty? That's the unusual question posed by this popular MMB class that incorporates the old Coca Cola theme song "I'd Like to Teach the World to Sing" into a surprising course coda. Required materials – Internet connection, lab jacket, iTunes

The Odd Farmer's Almanac for 2021

Albuquerque University Promotional Flyer

Theatrical Mathematics
TM 206: Primal Screaming, by the Numbers - A difficult message illustrating that all roots of inequality are mathematical in nature, but theatrical in expression, is presented in TM 206. Students in the course are encouraged to "act out," as they see fit, their deepest feelings about four being greater than three. No biting. No prerequisites. Awareness of fractions may be helpful.

Botanical English
BE 178: Care and Feeding of Weed - Unleash the pistils and free the stamens while exploring the literary perspective of Cannabis plant genitals! The spirit of Ken Kesey and the Merry Pranksters is alive and reaches new botanical "highs" in this wide-ranging discourse on plant sexual anatomy. Students will want to inhale deeply in the knowledge as instructors guide them through the writings of Mendel, Linnaeus, and O'Leary. Required materials – Miracle Gro™ and prescription or court order.

Geo-Religious Studies
GRS 246: Carbon Dating for the Self-Absorbed - He craves geology. She digs theology. Put them together and the results are, um, not exactly electrifying, if you get our "continental drift." Is geo-religion doomed to die out? Fear not. The latest offering from the GRS department is an exciting one credit course aimed at getting GeoReligious Studies majors to stare less at plate tectonics and holy books and more at each other. While satisfaction is not guaranteed, it is, ahem, not uncommon. Prerequisite – GRS 131 (The Richter Scale: Was it Good for You?)

Apparel Statistics
AS 249: Error Bars in Basic Black - Are see-through swimming suits the "next rage" or just another standard deviation? Does your butt look too big in those pants or is it a normal distribution? Taking inseam and other measurements to a new level, course instructors John von Neumann and Elle MacPherson allow even "least squares" to "fit" this data and learn why statistics is essential for success in today's clothing industry. Prerequisite – AS 184 (Chemise: Is That Gaussian or What?)

Modern Health Literature
MHL 202: A Man, A Plan, A Canal, Pain - Remember The Raven and The Telltale Heart? How about Jurassic Park and GATTACA? This intriguing new class asks the probing question "What would Edgar Allen Poe have to say about today's medical biotechnology?" and then, disturbingly, answers it. Can you say dentist-assisted-suicide? No prerequisites, but not for the faint of heart.

Spiritual Evolution
SE 327: Crock of Ages - First there was biological Darwinism, then social Darwinism. Ready for the next step in the process? You got it – religious Darwinism. SE 327 is an "intelligently designed" course that follows the major players as they exploit Darwinian principles of selection, niche exploitation, and survival of the fittest to evolve a doctrine that rules the earth.

The route to the porch light was passed on by word of moth

𝔗𝔥𝔢 𝔒𝔡𝔡 𝔉𝔞𝔯𝔪𝔢𝔯'𝔰 𝔄𝔩𝔪𝔞𝔫𝔞𝔠 𝔣𝔬𝔯 2021

Albuquerque University Promotional Flyer

Pity the meek. Prerequisite – Ape descendency, suspension of belief.

Home and Federal Economics
DE 308: For Sale by Renter - Inspired by Janet Yellen and the U.S. Department of Commerce, DE 308 is a night course aimed at working middle-class moms and dads hoping to apply principles of government spending to their family budgets. Course modules include "Let's Lease Lunch", "Outsourcing: The Children or The Laundry?", and the ever popular "How Much Down is the Little Audi in the Window?". Course requirement - Rational exuberance.

Political and Biophysical Sciences
PBS 301: Transformations in a Modern World: From Marx to Fourier. - A class that aims to reduce the signal to noise ratio in the media by applying Fourier transformations to Fox News reports, PBS 301 asks the biophysical/political question, "Can Mathematical Manipulation Lead to an Understanding of Ordered States of Crystallized Macromolecules and, if so, What About the Oppressed Masses?" Co-Requisite – PBS 302

Cellular Philosophy
MP 216: Hamlet's Multicellular Dilemma - Participate in a microbial mind game as professors lead students exploring the eternal, philosophical, cellular question, "To Be or To Go Into Apoptosis and Not Be?" Prerequisite – MP 201 (Shakespeare for Theoretical Botanists), MMB 333 (Mitotic Theory for English Majors)

Art Chemistry
AC 121: Ideal Gases: An Abstract Perspective - Introductory class restricted to Art Chemistry majors that asks the questions, 1) "Can the Works of Miro, Mondrian, Kandinsky, and Klae be Reduced to $PV = nRT$?" and 2) "What would Boyle have thought about those Kids with Big Eyes in 70s Art?" Prerequisite – AC 101 (Volume Theory for Art History Majors), open mind.

Psychology and Physics
PP 422: The Inertia of Freudian Slips - Does thinking too fast put the mind on an unstoppable path toward punning? Can rapid flux of sodium ions across neural gates in the cerebral cortex give uncontrollable and unanticipated insights into subconsciously perceived reality? Learn answers to these and other questions with big words in this seniors-only tag-team course. Prerequisite – PP 384 (From Hawking to Kant: Huh?)

Biochemical Dance
BD 418: Ribosomal Hip Hop - Join in the fun in the campus ballroom on Thursday evenings as students combine human kinetic sculpture with protein synthesis in the campus' newest course offering! Biochemistry professors and the Marysville Cloggers lead students, codon by codon down a messenger RNA on the dance floor to synthesize a fully functional enzyme. Music provided by the somnolent tunes of Nine Inch Nails. Prerequisite – BD 309 (Pilobus and Glycolysis)

Kids on merry-go-rounds remind us that wee are the whirled

The Odd Farmer's Almanac for 2021

Word Fun

The guy who has his hand up asking
Lots of questions knows
His friends think he is someone who's
A very big **askhole**

The judge gave his decision
And said, "Have no remorse"
"You guys are not a couple now"
"I give you a **dude-vorce**"

You're starting on a road trip and
Hand to your friend a Pepsi
But discover he's asleep
That guy has **car-colepsy**

What happens when a friend of yours
Spouts out a long narration?
And doesn't take input, of course
That is a **nonversation**

A demolition company
Can tear down your duplex
You have to give them credit for
Their sign, "**Edifice Wrecks**"

A roofing company took some heat
For a motto some assailed
"Hot Shingles in Your Area"
"All Looking to Get Nailed"

Don't look at me like I'm not here
Your narcissistic curse
Puts you alone all day in your
Own special **you-niverse**

If you should choose to go alone
To movies fascinating
The word that people give to that
Is simple - **masterdating**

Word Fun

If you're waiting for a message from
Someone and have temptation
To check it every minute you've
Contracted **textpectation**

State Farm Insurance has a guy
Who'll cover your home base
If you require his services
Go ask for **Justin Case**

You're at a seafood restaurant
And ordering some shellfish
Your date is on her phone and acting
Very, very **cell-fish**

You grab a book to learn about
A subject rather frightening
But didn't learn a thing because
The writing was **unlightening**

You walk the hall to get a pen
But suffer from amnesia
Why did you leave your office then?
A sign of **destinesia**

The metric system 'round the world
Leaves U.S. in seclusion
Does changing pounds to kilograms
Result in **mass confusion**?

Marital infidelity
Can cause depression scares
Wyoming has the most of these
A sad **state of affairs**

Into a store a duck did go
To get his Chapstick fill
When asked how he would pay for it
He said, "**Just put it on my bill**"

Great name for a plumbing business: "Seepless in Seattle"

Word Fun

My scientific article
On whales has been impeded
The journal called it incomplete
There were **cetaceans** needed

A writer lady I adored
Quizzed of my knowledge state
"Six letter word for 'calm?'," she asked
So I said, "**It's sedate**"

The patriot Paul upon his horse
Alerted people plenty
I think it is the reason why
He was **revered by many**

A baker bakes a lot of bread
But some he just discards
By stacking fifty two of those
He has a **deck of carbs**

Scotsmen with bagpipes shouldn't
Run with them atilt
Cuz they could put an eye out or
More likely they'd be **kilt**

The private eye named Mr. Holmes
Looked at a bed in shock
He said to Watson, "Something's gone"
The reply? "**No sheet Sherlock**"

A man who had a mane quite dark
Much craved ancestors fair
He dreamed of genealogy
That had some **light brown hair**

A leaker of the White House news
Has info that is prime
He's like a wound-up clock, they say
Cuz that's **when he tells Time**

Word Fun

A guy I know is one who's sought
Whenever things should fail
This patron saint of causes lost
Responds to **Noah Vail**

The baker has a lucky knife
I am big believer
When slicing several breads at once
It is a **four loaf cleaver**

Viking pharmacists practiced pillaging

It Will Get Better

The doors are locked and knobs are wiped
Overdue emails are getting typed
Forgotten friends long lost are Skyped
A virus is in town

Society is interrupted
Businesses have been disrupted
And smiles are certainly corrupted
Faces all have frowns

Spring's a time when we should be
Sitting underneath a tree
But we can't do that now, you see
A virus is in town

We've all got masks atop our faces
Avoiding all the public spaces
So we can't go too many places
Due to a lock down

But restaurants will fill once more
And people will go from door to door
Things will be just like they were before
That virus came to town

The Odd Farmer's Almanac for 2021

SEPTEMBER, 2021

Remember, back in the middle of January, when you were scraping the ice off the windshield of your car and that Arctic blast thought you were a wind tunnel? Summer sure sounded pretty great then, didn't it? And now, with the beginning of this month, it's the Labor Day holiday, the traditional end of the summer vacation period. Over the past three months, you've sweated buckets, peeled off a couple of pounds of fried, sunburned skin, strained muscles you didn't know existed, had heart arrhythmias induced by your air conditioning bill, gained more than twice the weight of the skin you flaked off, had a vacation that lasted all too short of a period of time, and you're ready for . . . . . a break from summer?

September is the start of a 9 month launch pad aimed at shooting us off into . . . next summer. It's well disguised in that role, at first taking us farther and farther away from the past summer until it is so far away we forget how uncomfortable, tired, cranky, and ready for it to be over that we were just a short time earlier. Fortunately, we have almanacs to remind us (writer bows).

You really don't want next summer. You'll be another year older and you'll feel just like you feel right now, at best. What you want is to enjoy each day as it comes for what it is and then to take it in to the fullest. But we both know you're about as likely to do that as you are to complete your new year's resolutions, which now have been ignored for 8 months since you "postponed" them. Resolutions have a statute of limitations, though, that removes all legal, civic, and moral obligations for completing them upon passing the 6 month mark, so NOBODY restarts them at this point of the year.

September carries us out of summer and delivers us into fall. It's the calendar singing lullabies to us, so it's only appropriate then that the month has its own song - and it does - "See You in September," written, recorded, and made popular in the span of about a week in 1959. Dozens of versions of the song have been recorded, from Debbie Boone to The Happenings.

> September is a popular month, music-wise. The oldest of these, "September Song," is an American standard, written in 1938, that compares one's life to a year and September is the time when days are getting shorter. It's a rare song recorded by both Willie Nelson and Frank Sinatra. "September" is one of the best known songs of Earth, Wind, and Fire. There's also a haunting instrumental "September Song" on piano played by Agnes Obel, and JP Cooper has a totally different and modern song entitled "September Song" as well.

September is also the month of the the fall season change. Although summer was over in most people's minds with the three day Labor day weekend, it actually doesn't end until the equinox, which occurs this year on September 22. In addition to the equinoxical event, there are the usual lunar gyrations - new (6th), half (13th), full (20th - Harvest Moon), and half (28th) and the usual rendezvous interactions between the moon and 1) Mercury (8th), 2) Venus (9th), 3) Saturn (16th), 4) Jupiter (17th), and 5) Uranus (24th). This month's meteor showers include the Aurugids (1st), minor Perseids (9th), and Sextantids (27th). ♫ See you in October ♫

The Odd Farmer's Almanac for 2021

September First
1904
Radcliffe College
Anxiously awaited
When Helen Keller
Graduated

September Second
1992
The U.S. and Russia
On this occasion
Agree to build
A space station

> I couldn't afford a fancy car, so I bought a Poorsche

September Third
1838
Disguised as a sailor
Exhibiting bravery
Frederick Douglass
Escapes slavery

September Fourth
1951
For the first time there
For all to see
A transcontinental broadcast
On TV

September Fifth
1889
Upholding principles
Near and dear
Christine Hardt
Patents the brassiere

> Planes that fly backward and forward are palindrones

Lily Tomlin born 9/1/1939

"People who fly into a rage always make a bad landing." - Will Rogers

> Guys too focused on their maleness are egotestical

September Sixth
1916
Charles Saunders
Hit it bigly
With the first supermarket
Piggly Wiggly

September Seventh
1909
Eugene Lefebvre
Made his name
The first pilot dying
In an airplane

September Eighth
1504
A naked man
Was unveiled
The Statue of David
Immediately hailed

September Ninth
1543
Mary Stuart
On the scene
Nine months old
And crowned the queen

September Tenth
2008
The Large Hadron Collider
Is finally transformed
The most expensive collisions
Earthlings performed

September Eleventh
1847
It was today
The catchy tune
O Susannah! debuted
In a Pittsburgh saloon

"When I eventually met Mr. Right I had no idea that his first name was Always" - Rita Rudner

The Odd Farmer's Almanac for 2021

September Twelfth
1873
Many would use it
To tell their tale
The first practical typewriter
To go on sale

September Thirteenth
1907
The Lusitania
Racing the waves
Crossed the Atlantic
In just five days

> **Bad fortune telling isn't prophetable**

September Fourteenth
1814
Francis Scott Key
Saw bombs burst in air
And wrote up an anthem
About a flag still up there

September Fifteenth
1928
Recognizing
Bacterial killin'
Alexander Fleming
Discovered penicillin

September Sixteenth
1983
Seeing where
It might take him
Arnold Schwarzenegger
Became a U.S. citizen

September Seventeenth
1683
van Leeuwenhoek's new
Microscope tool
Shows him bacteria
He dubbed "animalcules"

"Clothes make the man. Naked people have little or no influence on society." - Mark Twain

> **I dropped my bowl of Alpha-bits cereal and cried over spelt milk**

September Eighteenth
1851
The New York Times
Did this day commence
Its publishing
The cost? Two cents

September Nineteenth
1970
She'd "light the world up with her smile"
And rode it to great success
The Mary Tyler Moore Show
Premiered on CBS

September Twentieth
1973
A victory for women
Over a chauvinist pig
Billy Jean King
Defeats Bobby Riggs

September Twenty First
1897
Although 'twasn't Christmas
It gave no one pause
When the New York Sun printed
"Yes Virginia, There is a Santa Claus"

> **Invisible lettuce - Romaines to be seen**

September Twenty Second
1989
Never a show
With great reviews
But on this day
"Baywatch" debuts

A KFC diet means biting the pullet

The Odd Farmer's Almanac for 2021

Lawngevity - The number of days you can go between mowings

September Twenty Third
1806
After three years gone
Lewis and Clark earn
A boisterous celebration
Of many happy returns

September Twenty Fourth
1934
The Bambino was
A great big guy
And today Babe Ruth
Told New York fans goodbye

September Twenty Fifth
1513
Vasco Balboa crossing Panama
Was an explorer in motion
Becoming the first European
To see the Pacific Ocean

September Twenty Sixth
1957
The Sharks and the Jets, they had a fight
Fortunately it wasn't gory
Instead it was just opening day
For a play called "West Side Story"

September Twenty Seventh
1905
It was on this day
That Einstein shared
His famous equation
E = MC squared

I dreamed of installing a window, but couldn't handle the pane

"People who fly into a rage always make a bad landing" - Will Rogers

Reruns are deja viewed

September Twenty Eighth
1066
William the Conquerer
Of pillaging fame
Invades England
Living up to his name

September Twenty Ninth
1953
Lotsa jokes
Never filthy
Today's premiere?
Uncle Miltie

September Thirtieth
1859
Though its earliness seems
A little bit strange
George Simpson patents
The electric range

The fruit seller decided to not make a fuss and kumquatly

Mel Brooks born 9/28/1926

"The Flintstones" debut 9/30/60

"You know you've reached middle age when you're cautioned to slow down by your doctor, instead of by the police."
—Joan Rivers

"Someone asked me, if I were stranded on a desert island what book would I bring: 'How to Build a Boat.'"
—Steven Wright

"Folks, I don't trust children. They're here to replace us."
– Stephen Colbert

Page 80

The Odd Farmer's Almanac for 2021

Timely Matters

I went to bed too late last night
And woke up to an awful fright
But now it's done, what can I say?
Tomorrow somehow became today

They say time flies, you never know
About the days, where do they go?
A penny in your pocket, say
Keep it, spend it, that's OK

But time displayed upon your clock
Is not an item you can stock
It can't be captured, stored away
Or used to fill another day

It just slips forward, always runs
Quantized by the setting suns
It stops for no one, people say
And when it goes, it's gone away

There's Father Time and Mother Goose
One's for kids and one's a noose
New Year's baby, Old Man Time
Champagne maybe, aging wine

You can have a sec or take a minute
Lose it in spring, in fall re-win it
The clock is ticking all the time
Tick tock talking on your dime

You can spend some time to learn guitar
If it's on your side, you may go far

Or not

And you can have it on your hands
But not upon your feet
It may fly by on the weekends, but
Be dragging in the week

Power outages are delightful

Timely Matters

Time is money, so they say
But it is such a crime
That money comes and goes away
But never turns to time

And in good time, we all will die
As all the days go pass us by
But no one has the answer why
Time keeps marching on

Yes, you can die before your time
But never after it, you see
It can be a most untimely thing
But timely death will never be

The sands of time make silent chorus
Dropping down the glass before us
Slipping, running, marching fast
Turning present into past

Just one more thing, before I go
To end this longish shout
I need to bum some change, because
My meter's running out

**Smiling
increases your face value**

Urine Trouble Now

My puppy isn't potty trained
I'll be glad when that is done
But up til then, I need to be
Looking out for number one

And depending on what
This dog might do
I must also try
To avoid number two

Anagrams

A DORMITORY is a place
To which all students zoom
But rearrange the letters and
You get a DIRTY ROOM

Recall GEORGE BUSH the younger
His race left many sore
Some say it's true right to this day
That HE BUGS GORE

The SNOOZE ALARMS mean sleeping
You can push as oft you please
But if you do that you should know
It means "ALAS NO MORE Z'S"

I see there is A DECIMAL POINT
Inside that number's space
It said what it was doing there
That "I'M A DOT IN PLACE"

Carl Sagan the ASTRONOMER
Looked upwards more his share
Perhaps that is the reason why
They called him a MOON STARER

SLOT MACHINES are evil things
I think it's plain to see
They all should have a sign on them
That says CASH LOST IN ME

In DESPERATION, suicide's
So sad, no one defends it
There's many ways that you can go
Remember A ROPE ENDS IT

THE MORSE CODE you don't see
much now
Though once it got used lots
Each time a message would arrive
You'd know HERE COME DOTS

Anagrams

ELECTION RESULTS
May wrack your nerves
About the true amount
A standard line in races close
Is "LIES, LET'S RECOUNT"

Your MOTHER-IN-LAW
may not be great
But please do not be bitter
You'll probably make an enemy
By calling her WOMAN HITLER

I am afraid of EARTHQUAKES and
I'm not a big snowflake
It's just that when we have one
It gives me THAT QUEER SHAKE

A PRESBYTERIAN on his knees
Is not so very rare
I've heard a claim they are the ones
Who are the BEST IN PRAYER

And finally to close it out
Before this verse is done
I'll tell you that ELEVEN PLUS TWO
Is the same as TWELVE PLUS ONE

Too Much Time

I got arrested the other day
Seems what I did was not OK

An officer told me that my crime
Was I had taken too much time

"But what," I said, "I didn't know"
"That it was time for me to go"

"Ignorance," he said, "is no excuse"
"You mess with time and you will lose"

Because of this, it seems that I'm
A person who'll be doing time

The Odd Farmer's Almanac for 2021

More Double Meanings

Relief can feel so good that it
Just makes you stop and sing
And also what a maple does
When it encounters spring

You **rubberneck** to look at things
Because of your sex drive
And also what you do when you
Work to relax your wife

Our **President** leads the country
Protecting me and you
And also is the work that many
Auto fixers do

You're **selfish** if you hoard your things
And want to give no more
And also what you do when you
Are running a fish store

Take **Sudafed** for congestion
It's money quite well spent
And also what you do when seeking
Damage from government

Billowing is what your sails will do
If they should catch some breezes
And also what will go up when
Indebtedness increases

A fashionable Doberman is an avant guard dog

Common Frustration
With COVID, it is maddening
That the learning curve
Is the only thing flattening
While everything else
Just seems to be fattening

Facebooked

The look in your eyes
Vacant, bereft
As if there is
No person left

The search for approval
Never ceasing
Always striving
Craving pleasing

What happened to
The one I knew?
It seems you've come
Unhooked

That selfie smile
The "perfect" you
Sadly
You're Facebooked

Doing Time
We're prisoners to the phone
And you can tell
That's why we say that
It's a cell

The Stables Have Turned

One hundred years ago memoirs
Recorded in history courses
That richest folks would drive in cars
And others rode on horses

But as we all fast forward - wow!
Today, we've come quite far
The rich ones ride on horses now
And average Joes drive cars

Guardin' Eden

I love to walk most every day
Along the road down Campus Way

Out through the covered bridge I stroll
In wind and rain and fog and snow

The countryside. The gentle breeze
Herons, pastures, many trees

Hawks and kestrels in the skies
Summertime and butterflies

Joggers jog and bluebirds cheep
Dr. Stormshak tends his sheep

I love this place, it feeds my soul
The sky, the land, each rabbit hole

No nearby place that I'm aware of
Deserves to be better taken care of

For Daniel

Now Daniel, though I know your name
I don't know you, but just the same
I write for you this science verse
I hope that it is not the worst

We scientists have education
But also quite a reputation
Of being nerds, but that's now cool
So you should work real hard in school

Resolve to work in this school year
To get a jump on your career
It's better spending time with books
Than wasting efforts on one's looks

Cuz looks will fade with increased aging
So hard to know with hormones raging
But that's just Mother Nature's ways
So study science - get those A's

The Little Kitty

I found a little kitty
It followed me one day

I had a lot of fun with it
I loved to watch it play

My laser light astounded it
A ball of yarn it chased

The world was one big mystery
That cat was so amazed

And all was well until today
While playing with some socks

The little kitty fell into
A giant moving box

That folded up and closed itself
The kitten deep inside

Perhaps it's happy in the fact
It has a place to hide

Or maybe it has perished
Just one way to decide

Ah, Schrodinger!

Traitor Joe

Yesterday morning
My friend intervened
Cuz when I don't get my coffee
I'm such a caffiend

But then I got served
At nine fifteen
And quickly turned into
A big has bean

The Odd Farmer's Almanac for 2021

Dog Breeding

A Bloodhound and a Lab when crossed
Would be hard to ignore
It probably would not shut up
A noisy **Blabrador**

A Dalmation and a Malamute
Would make an odd creation
There is a chance it might be odd
Since it is a **Mutation**

A collie and a Lhaso Apso
Should I breed them? Perhaps so
I'd get a dog that I could fold
Since it would be a **Collapso**

But what if I should dare to cross
A pointer and a setter?
'Twould surely make a Yuletide gift
That's known as a **Poinsetter**

An Irish Setter and Springer Spaniel
Would make a soapy thing
That you might use inside your bath
Cuz you'd have **Irish Spring**

A Terrier and a Bulldog would
Sure be a cross to mull
On second thought I am afraid
It might be **Terribull**

A Bulldog and a Shitzhu crossed
Is a bad idea, don't do it
Because the offspring they produce
Would surely make a **BullShit**

An art collector tried to cross
A Pekingese and Lhasa Apso
So she would have her very own
Version of **Peekasso**

Legal marijuana is a big hit

A Tale of Two Fishies

Just yesterday I had a wish
To eat a little tunie fish

This dream of tasty albacore
Led me down to the grocery store

Upon arriving on aisle three
I found my Chicken of the Sea

Or so I thought 'til I got back
And looked inside the grocery sack

Twas then I realized with terror
The grievous nature of my error

Beside the Reynolds cooking foil
Was tunie fish in cans of oil

I'll feed it to my Siamese
So I don't plug the arteries

Next time I go to shop I gotta
Buy tunie fish in cans of watta

Facebook is clique bait

Homonysms

We apologize to you oh my dear deer
For the rather horrid racket you hear here
But our brand new subdivision
Advertised on television
Isn't going very soon to disappear

We are very sorry you are now bare bear
Having just removed your very hairy hair
For a rug upon our floor
That the neighbors will adore
Each and every single time that they're there

The Odd Farmer's Almanac for 2021

OCTOBER, 2021

October is the tenth month of our year and "Oct," of course, means eight so, uh. Hmmm. There actually is a logic to it and those of you who have been paying close attention to these monthly epistles can figure it out. Hint - it comes from the Romans. Another hint - the calendar isn't the same as it always was. Last hint - the Roman calendar started with March (go figure). Yes, yes, you brilliant hint taker you, October was the 8th month in the Roman calendar and only later, after January and February were added, did October become the 10th month. September (Sep = 7), November (Nov = 9) and December (Dec = 10) have the same Roman roots as October.

How do you have a calendar missing two months of the year? Leap months. That's right. You know that expression "spring forward and fall back?" It actually comes from the Romans who liked the fall months so much they would sometimes repeat them and it actually helped to keep their calendar aligned. Though it wreaked havoc for people like almanac makers, historians, astrologers, wedding planners, and (Latin) word-of-the-day creators, it worked great for procrastinators of all kinds, like last minute Christmas shoppers, homework doers, and renters ("But I paid you for October's rent - here's my receipt"). Fortunately, Roman lawns didn't grow in the fall months

Though you may think I made that last paragraph up (I did), there is one thing about it that rings true - Roman leap months are the reason why people today still discuss the Fall of the Roman Empire.

Okaaaaay. Moving on, October 1 is also the time that the federal fiscal year starts. Why a date so late in the calendar year was chosen for this momentous annual beginning is unknown, due to the fact that the person who actually knew the reason wrote it down on a piece of paper, which was subsequently lost in the federal bureaucracy. Perhaps they should have stuck it to a piece of red tape (HAR!).

October also provides us with Halloween, which is (HAR again!) the official beginning of the Pumpkin Spice Latte (PSL) season. Currently, no one is legally allowed to order a PSL before October 31, but, if PSL season goes like Christmas season has gone (54 shopping days left by Halloween), the PSL buying will soon begin on Memorial Day because, why not? Curiously, the same thing never happened for egg nog. Maybe not so curious - the problem with ordering an egg nog is that it carries a risk you may have to drink it - blecccccccch.

October also brings us astronomy which, by now, you realize happens every month, and October is definitely a month, as established above. To actually BE different, let's start October astronomy with meteor showers. The names are great - Carmelopardalids flare on the 5th. The Draconids (think DRACULA) are on the 8th, Geminids on the 18th, Orionids on the 21st, and Leonis Minorids on the 24th. That's a lot of showers - hopefully you won't meteor maker (HAR! #3). The moon mostly exhibits social distancing this month, making close approaches only to Venus (9th), Saturn (14th), and Jupiter (15th). Phase-wise, you can see it go new (6th), half (12th), full (20th), and half (28th). And, finally, as the mathematicians say at this time of year, Happy "Trig or Treat."

The Odd Farmer's Almanac for 2021

October First
1891
Stanford U's first day was today
A place for shakers and movers
Its first student was notable
Future President, Herbert Hoover

October Second
1866
J. Osterhoudt was really
A very important man
Inventing an opener
After someone made the tin can

> Peer pressure - what guys sometimes feel at urinals

October Third
1955
A great day for kids
Two TV shows debut
Disney's Mickey Mouse Club
And Captain Kangaroo

October Fourth
1959
Many years before Gary Larson
Ever hit his stride
The first pictures arrived
Of the moon's far side

October Fifth
1977
No other musical
Could compare
To the stripped down version
Of "Hair"

> Smoky the Bear says you should respect your alders

"The Jerk" debut 10/2/2001
Charlie Brown debut - 10/4/1950
Monty Python debut - 10/5/1969
Wallace & Gromit debut - 10/5/2005

> Egotists get me-deep in conversation

October Sixth
1966
California
Surprisingly
The first to ban
LSD

October Seventh
1916
Cumberland College
Hit the wall
Losing 222-0
In college football

October Eighth
1906
Distresses over tresses
No longer a care
With the invention of
Permanent waves for hair

October Ninth
1992
A meteor exploded overhead
It was quite a sight to view
Lest you owned what one piece destroyed
A Chevy Malibu

October Tenth
1886
A dinner jacket worn this day
Was a first, but please don't smirk
Its name came from where 'twas worn
Tuxedo Park, New York

October Eleventh
1975
With George Carlin as host
And a whole lot of work
Saturday Night Live premieres
With "Live from New York!"

"Why do they call it rush hour when nothing moves?" - Robin Williams

Tie dye sales are hippie hunting grounds

The Odd Farmer's Almanac for 2021

October Twelfth
1492
After a long ocean voyage
Of considerable duration
Columbus arrives
At a non-Asian nation

October Thirteenth
1792
Helping farmers
To keep on track
Robert Thomas publishes
"*The Old Farmer's Almanac*"

October Fourteenth
1892
Mysteries aplenty
Please don't spoil
Sherlock Holmes is published by
Arthur Conan Doyle

> I put on the flimsy gown in the hospital and everyone said "ICU"

October Fifteenth
1860
Not liking
The way he appeared
Grace Bedell tells Lincoln
To grow a beard

October Sixteenth
1384
Poland has a new king
But there's more to this tale
The subject of this story
Is Jadwiga, a female

October Seventeenth
1933
As needy as he
Could possibly be
Einstein arrives
A German refugee

Mad Magazine debut October, 1952

"Young Frankenstein" debut 10/15/1974

Oscar Wilde born 10/16/1854

October Eighteenth
1931
Al Capone
On this occasion
Got his only conviction
For tax evasion

> Two volcanologists fell in lava with each other

October Nineteenth
1901
A musical piece
To which graduates prance
Edward Elgar's
"Pomp and Circumstance"

October Twentieth
1911
Mr. Amundsen racing southward
Had good luck, I am told
The South Pole was the prize
A good set of dice he Roald

October Twenty First
1797
Resistant to both
Cannons and tides
The U.S. launches
Old Ironsides

> I squeezed a sponge ball too hard and got Nerf damage

October Twenty Second
1861
A full east-west telegraph line
The U.S. acquired
The very first time
It would be wired

Eight of the ten largest statues in the world are of Buddhas.

Page 88

The Odd Farmer's Almanac for 2021

October Twenty Third
1814
At the time
They thought it fantastic
When performing the very first
Surgery plastic

Biblical fortune tellers are psalm readers

October Twenty Fourth
1818
Felix Mendelssohn
Musically inclined
Performs his first concert
At the age of nine

October Twenty Fifth
1870
The very first postcard
Brought vacation cheer
"Having great time"
"Wish you were here"

Dracula was a hemosexual

October Twenty Sixth
1858
A big advance
To keep clothes clean
Hamilton Smith patents
Rotary washing machines

October Twenty Seventh
1925
Fun devices
For rivers, lakes, and the seas
Fred Waller patents
Water skis

No monsters are good at math unless you Count Dracula

October Twenty Eighth
1886
The Statue of Liberty dedicated
For all to see
Followed by the first
Parade with confetti

October Twenty Ninth
1945
Enabling the writing
Of many a tale
The first ballpoint pen
Goes on sale

October Thirtieth
1938
A massive panic
Rapidly unfurls
With the Orson Welles' hoax
"The War of the Worlds"

October Thirty First
1941
In South Dakota
Of all places
Mt. Rushmore opens
Revealing four faces

Halloween ghosts practice Boodism

Dracula was a red blood cell Count

John Cleese born 10/27/1939

Public Servants

Elections are what politicians
Always have to stand for
And politicians are the things
That voters seem to fall for

Yes, this is true
There is no doubt
They get sworn in
And then cursed out

Page 89

The Odd Farmer's Almanac for 2021

My Ghost Story

Everyone has ghost stories. They always seem to involve someone who knew someone who was related to someone, etc. How many people have an actual personal ghost story to tell? Well, I'm one of those people.

My ghost story took place over the span of 30 years, so please bear with me. As you may recall, I grew up in rural Illinois. One of the main activities for young boys there was baseball. Little League (under 12 years of age) and Pony League (12-16) were how a good percentage of our summer evenings were occupied. My younger brother and I lived and breathed baseball for the first 16 years of our lives. When the movie called Field of Dreams came out, watching it was like going home. All rural baseball diamonds in Illinois are next to corn fields.

Baseball gave me many friendships, one of which was with a young man named Curt Sellers. Curt was one of the most likable people I ever knew and he was an incredible athlete to boot. He was three years older than me and we played baseball together one summer in Coatsburg, Illinois. My parents, who went to all of the Coatsburg Colts games, LOVED Curt.

When I say I came from rural Illinois, I mean VERY rural. Our town was so tiny that it took 5 similar towns together to have enough kids for a high school, Unity High, which was located in Mendon, Illinois.

When I started at Unity, Curt was one of the few upperclassmen who didn't get his jollies picking on freshmen like me and he was a great friend. Everyone liked Curt, and with good reason. I always remember him asking about my parents. Clearly he liked them as well. Curt was the everything athlete at Unity - baseball, track, and was a star basketball player.

As I noted, freshmen at Unity got a fair amount of abuse from older students for no other reason than they had gotten the same when they were freshmen and it was time to "pay it backward." As a result, apart from Curt, my friends were mostly freshmen and one of those was a young man named Phil Smith. Like me, Phil was a kind of geeky young man who wore the same kind of awkward, black framed glasses I wore. In looking back, I see myself as being very closed minded, but Phil was the opposite, open to other answers and not being afraid to question. He also knew how to talk to girls, something I was a long ways from mastering at that young age.

Within two years of each other and one year after graduating from high school, while still in their teens, Curt and Phil, each succumbed to cancer. Phil had a bit more warning, with leukemia that he was treated for unsuccessfully for 2-3 years. Curt, on the other hand, had an advanced cancer discovered way too late to do anything about it and he was gone before many even knew he was sick. For the first time in my life, I knew people who weren't old who had died. It still makes me sick to think about it.

Fast forward from the early 70s to about 2000. By this time, I was a professor and academic advisor at Oregon State University. One of the students I served as advisor to was a young woman named Janine (name changed for privacy). Janine was a bright,

My Ghost Story

talented and poised young woman who loved horses. I was working in my office one afternoon when I got a strange email message written all in lower case and without any punctuation saying something like "this is janine im in the hospital." Since I knew several Janines in the large class I was teaching at the time, I wasn't quite sure whom it was from or if it was some kind of a joke. After a couple of weird exchanges, I realized it was my advisee, Janine and she had a serious problem.

Janine, it had turned out, had had an aneurysm in her brain that burst while was riding her horse a few days earlier, giving her a stroke at the age of 19. Fortunately, someone saw her fall from the horse, called an ambulance, and got her to a hospital. The results of the stroke meant that the right side of her body was basically paralyzed and she was having trouble using her computer to communicate with me. I was shocked and, of course, offered to help her in any way I could with academic matters while she recovered. I'll never forget seeing her when she was released from the hospital. She came to my office sort of stumbling and with one corner of her mouth hanging low due to the paralysis. She could barely walk and struggled to talk.

There was a very happy ending to Janine's story, though. At the age of 19, one's brain is flexible enough that it can re-learn much of what it needs to. Over the next few months with a LOT of work, Janine slowly recovered all of her lost functions. If you were to look at her today, you would see no obvious evidence of the trauma she had suffered. I went to her wedding years later and delighted in watching her dance with her husband at the event. Such a happy day that was.

So, you might be wondering, where is the ghost story? That came about a year after Janine's accident, while she was still at OSU. Janine came to my office one day all worried. Her news was that she was going to transfer to another school to complete her degree, specifically the University of Oregon, OSU's arch rival, and she wanted me to know and to say goodbye. Students often think I'll be upset by their changing of schools, so I, of course, reassured her that I was happy for her and I knew she would do great at her new school and while I would certainly miss her, I would always be in her corner.

In saying goodbye to Janine, I told her how inspiring her recovery story was to me and, as I did this, my thoughts turned to Phil and Curt - each Janine's age when they had died. I told her their tragic stories and how, after 30 years, it still bothered me, but that working with her and watching her regain all of her abilities made me very happy. Here in front of me was a 19 year old who had faced death as Curt and Phil had, but unlike them, she had escaped its horrible embrace.

I remember very emotionally telling Janine that she was going to have the life that neither of them had had the chance to and I wanted her to live it to the fullest. I gave her a hug as she left and I sat back in my chair with tears in my eyes, emotionally exhausted. As I was sitting there reflecting and trying to compose myself, a young man from the class I was teaching knocked on my door and asked if he could pick up his exam. Since it was a large class, I apologized because I didn't know his name by looking at his face. His name was Phil Smith.

Kevin's Rules of Writing

1. Always. Avoid. Unnecessary. Punctuation.
2. Its best to alway's use apostrophe's properly.
3. Speling maters.
4. Use the write words at all times.
5. Don't forget to put a period at the end of a sentence otherwise you will confuse people
6. Make sure all sentences a verb
7. Use exclamation points sparingly!!!!!!!!!!!
8. When you write a dependent clause that needs another segment to complete a sentence,
9. Don't be a dumb ass - vulgar words should never be used in good writing.
10. When you're writing, you know, I think it is important, no matter what else you do, such as daydreaming, eating, drinking (all kinds of activities) or if you aren't sure what you want to say or even if you are sure what you want to say, but you don't know how to say it, you should always (or almost always) be concise and get to the point quickly.
11. Never write in absolutes.
12. Casual language has no place in formal writing, ya know?
13. Abbr. should not be used.
14. Don't start sentences you can't
15. Right order words put the in

The Lady Bug

A lady bugged a lady bug out sunning in the garden
When realizing what she'd done, she begged the insect's pardon

"I'm sorry to be bothering you. Please do not take offense"
"But I have planned a party here and gone to great expense"

The lady bug packed up her things to seek another yard
A rather lengthy journey - for a lady bug, that's hard!

The lady who was bugging her saw how she was imposing
And told the little lady bug, "Don't worry, I'm supposing"

"That it would be much easier for me to move than you"
"So I shall find another place to take my party to

The lady bug was happy then, she'd get to keep her castle
For the lady who'd been bugging her relieved a major hassle

Remember little lady bugs, when building subdivisions
And consequences unintended from all those decisions

The Odd Farmer's Almanac for 2021

Fall Leaves

It is that time when
Leaves are fallin'
And old man winter's
Voice starts callin'

Here in October
Things move slower
Except around
Those big leaf blowers

There's cookies splashed with
Orangish icing
And everything has
Pumpkin spicing

Having passed
The equinox
'Twill soon be time
To turn back clocks

There's ghosts and goblins
In the streets
Who come requesting
Tricks or treats

This time of year
Would have perfection
Except for just this
One objection

I guess it may seem
Treasonous
To bring it up
And make a fuss

But I confess
The truth is I'm
Not ready yet
For Christmas time

Spicy hot south Asian food leaves one tongue Thai'd

The Tree Searchin'

To the farm I rode
Upon my bike
To get a tree
My dogwood like

My budget's tight
So I am focussed
On getting one
That's very locust

When I got there
I felt unease
Could not cedar forest
For the trees

So now I think I'll
Wait til I'm
Ready to pecan
Other one some time

In sum, those things
Are what I'd do
That's my advice
From me to yew

Mighty Mouth

"Almighty God does not roll dice"
So Albert Einstein said
But does he think of naughty/nice
Inside his Godly head?

Methinks some words got scrambled
When the messages arrived
Cuz Moses had too many things
Stored on his hard rock drive

Birds go on pecknics

"Every man is guilty of all the good he did not do."
– Voltaire

Page 93

I've Had It With English

I've had it with English
So please hear my rant
Why is there no egg
Inside an eggplant?

About a pineapple
I just have to whine
You won't find an apple
And there's no trace of pine

Plus in a hamburger
There's nary a gram
Of anything like
The meat of a ham

Fortunately, though
In this monologue
There's no trace of canine
Inside a hot dog

At big boxing rings
I can't help but swear
Because they're not round
Instead they are square

If a boxer can box
And a spammer can spam
Then how come a hammer
Is unable to ham?

If a writer can write
And a singer can sing
Then what about fingers
Why can't they fing?

If you get in quicksand
Then you need to know
You will not sink quickly
In fact, it is slow

A nose might start running
Anytime you're unwell
But it's rather crazy
Your two feet can smell

I've Had It With English

If you should offend
A very good friend
You go make amends
Why not an amend?

If vegetarians eat vegetables
And shun all that meat
Please tell me then what should
Humanitarians eat?

You play at a recital
On a bright and sunny day
So why do you then
Recite at a play?

You put cargo on ships
Paying many a buck
But if you go shipping things
They travel by truck

A slim chance and fat chance
Are the same, it's the pits
But wise men and wise guys
Are exact opposites

And what is the thinking
In this crazy town
Each house that burns up
Also burns down

If you should apply
To join the Cub Scouts
You'll fill in a form
By filling it out

And how does a colorfast
Fabric get done?
It sounds very speedy
But it will not run

These are all things
That my teachers have taught
I can't be a squeacher
Cuz I don't know squaught

Mr. Potatohead was the first toy advertised on TV

The Odd Farmer's Almanac for 2021

NOVEMBER, 2021

So now that we've reached November, all U.S. citizens are required to use the word "holidays" at least once in every conversation until Christmas (24 holiday shopping days left at the end of the month). No amount of denying or ignoring it, is going to make the season go away, not that you would want to, Mr. or Ms Scrooge.

Moving to standard time is the first big holiday prep event of the month on the 7th. Don't forget to set those clocks back an hour. Before doing so, it would pay to check and be sure that the clock you are setting back is not one of those "self-setting" ones. A holiday prep you might want to try is a good "fall back" technique for the next two months. Go into your bathroom, grab your scale, and set it back about 20 pounds. Though you won't be any lighter, it's almost certain you'll smile the next you hop on it, especially if you wait a while and forget about the "turning back" thing. Remember, feeling good is what the holidays are all about, so by doing this, you're getting into the "spirit of the season."

While you're at it, some other things you might consider turning back - the calendar (50 is the new 70, right?), your car's odometer (the major reason they say "your mileage may vary"), and last, don't forget to turn back the Tide. Now this last one may seem like a cheap, gratuitous attempt at humor, but it is actually a holiday safety announcement/reminder based on the fact that the words on the back of each box of Tide pods saying "Not for human consumption" are there for purposes other than decoration.

There. With all of that preparation, you're now officially ready for the centerpiece event of the month, a time when people of all races, creeds, colors, religions, and nationalities gather together in family units around tables to count their blessings, celebrate a bountiful harvest and map out the best route to take to the Black Friday sales. Yes, Black Friday, of course, has become so much a part of our Thanksgiving celebration that the Union of Concerned Turkeys is proposing the day previously known as Thanksgiving be formally replaced by the sales events that follow it. In many "big box" stores (and families of the people unfortunate enough to work in them), it already has, with Black Friday sales curiously starting on Thursday, to "get a jump on" the holiday sale season. That, in itself, is odd, inasmuch as mailboxes have been bulging with catalogs announcing the beginning of the holiday shopping season since about July 4th. When the holiday shopping season actually starts is yet another of those mysteries of the universe Albert Einstein was working on furiously at the time of his death. We may never know.

What we do know, though, is that holiday sales aren't the only things astronomic in November. There is, for example, the moon, which is not technically for sale (yet), but IS new (3rd), half (11th), full (19th), and halved again (27th) all within the month. It cozies up to Mercury (4th), Venus (7th), Saturn (10th), and Jupiter (11th) in its monthly sky meanderings. A couple of meteor showers may be the highlights of the month. They are the Taurids on the 12th and the Leonids on the 17th. Fortunately, there are no meteor showers, eclipses, occultations, or other significant celestiality on Black Friday (26th), so early morning shoppers won't be distracted from their missions by looking up at at the sky and losing their places in line.

The Odd Farmer's Almanac for 2021

November First
1800
John Adams
Along with his spouse
The first Prez to occupy
The White House

November Second
1898
With Johnny Campbell
As the ringleader
A football crowd'
Has its first cheerleader

> Too much fishing causes cirrhosis of the river

> **With respect to rising sea levels, it's the thawed that counts**

November Third
1913
Because so many
Women had kvetched
Mary Phelps Jacob patented
The first bra that stretched

November Fourth
1841
With nothing to lose
And everything to gain
The first arrivals in California
By wagon train

November Fifth
1935
Staking out
Their claim to fame
Parker Brothers releases
The Monopoly game

November Sixth
1928
Known for his work
As a whisker grazer
Jacob Schick patents
The electric razor

> Will Rogers born 11/4/1879

> **Engagement has a nice ring to it**

November Seventh
1805
An event packed with
A lot of emotion
Lewis and Clark spot
The Pacific Ocean

November Eighth
1731
An American
Exemplary
Ben Franklin opens
Our first library

November Ninth
1620
After two months at sea
They thought it was grand
When the Mayflower crew
Spotted first land

November Tenth
1951
Perhaps it was due
To user insistence
The first long distance call
Without operator assistance

> **Income tax is capital punishment**

November Eleventh
1933
The "Black Blizzard"
Covered cars and trains
The first big dust storm
On the great plains

> What is Averagecalifragilisticexpialidociousness?

> **Atheists have no invisible means of support**

Page 96

The Odd Farmer's Almanac for 2021

November Twelfth
1933
Nessie they call him
Near the Loch, if you care
The first pic ever taken
Of something not there

If Disney made War and Peace, they would call it "TolStory"

November Thirteenth
1789
Reflecting on
His olden days
Ben Franklin wrote his famous
Death and taxes phrase

November Fourteenth
1910
Though it really wasn't
Too much of a trip
Today the first flight
Occurred from a ship

November Fifteenth
1904
King C. Gillette
Guess what he made?
Patents the first
Gillette razor blade

Great name for a tree surgeon business - "Poplar Mechanics"

November Sixteenth
1841
The first life preservers
Were made in New York
Interestingly enough
They were made of cork

"The health of nations is more important than the wealth of nations." - Will Rogers

November Seventeenth
1913
The shortcut certainly
Boosted sailor morale
When the first ship passed through
The Panama Canal

November Eighteenth
1307
Just inches away
From killing him dead
William Tell nails an apple
Atop his son's head

November Nineteenth
1959
Ford cancelled the Edsel
It lives in infamy
And Rocky and Bullwinkle
Premiered on TV

November Twentieth
1982
Nine years before
She was able to drive
Seven year old Drew Barrymore
Hosted Saturday Night Live

November Twenty First
1967
Phil and Jane Kunz
With string were replete
Setting kite height records
28,000 feet

November Twenty Second
1927
Notable for moving
With no visible wheel
Carl Eliason patents
The snowmobile

Coffee plantation workers are grounds keepers

Imogene Coca born 11/18/1908

Veterinarians are Dogtors

> **Everything is relative, but relatives aren't everything**

November Twenty Third
1921
President Harding
Had just had his fill
Signing the Willis-Campbell Act
The anti-beer bill

November Twenty Fourth
1971
A hijacker went
And jumped from a plane
Then disappeared
D.B. Cooper, his name

November Twenty Fifth
1867
Alfred Nobel
Of prize fame, tonight
Received a patent
For dynamite

November Twenty Sixth
1896
Alonzo Stagg
His opponents befuddled
Creates the first
Football huddle

November Twenty Seventh
1911
In a first for a group
Of U.S. detractors
The audience throws vegetables
At a group of bad actors

> **The riverboat got lost and went saline in the ocean**

"Worrying is like paying on a debt that may never come due." - Will Rogers

November Twenty Eighth
1893
A New Zealand election
Is worthy of note
The world's first big one
In which women can vote

November Twenty Ninth
1935
Erwin Schrödinger
Is a physicist that
Doesn't know very much
Of the state of his cat

November Thirtieth
1924
Information transfer
Reaches a max
When the Atlantic no longer
Is a barrier to fax

Mark Twain born 11/30/1835

> **When curling irons stop working, do they become hair straighteners?**

"The only reason some people get lost in thought is because it's unfamiliar territory."
– Paul Fix

"I want my children to have all the things I couldn't afford. Then I want to move in with them."
– Phyllis Diller

"Never put off till tomorrow what you can do the day after tomorrow."
– Mark Twain

The Odd Farmer's Almanac for 2021

Tom Swiftie Verses

"My lady friend did not show up"
"I guess romance is dead"
"It hurts me most inside my chest"
Half-heartedly Tom said

"My family has changed a lot"
"Especially father Ted:
"Who wants to go by Tina now,"
As she transparently said

"They've stolen all the lamps we have"
My father just recited
I guess that is the reason why
He's sounding so delighted

My kitten makes me feel so good
When my condition's chronic
I wondered why and asked my doc
"So is this catatonic?"

Tom couldn't talk to her back then
And that left her appalled
She's phoning him again right now
The lady just recalled

Blowing air beneath a roof
Can cool dramatically
"I like its high efficiency"
Said Tom, fanatically

The Realtor

My realtor friend
Just likes to say
She does a good deed
Every day

And she's the one
To go and find
If you've a lot
On your mind

Tom Swiftie Verses

"The orca for our show tonight"
"Has sadly been impaled"
"I don't think there's another one"
The Sea World owner wailed

The line inside the clinic caused
Most people there to groan
"I don't mind waiting for the Doc"
Tom patiently intoned

"He rammed his car into mine twice"
"It wasn't very subtle"
"Perhaps I'll do the same to him"
Replied Tom in rebuttal

They gave to him a lot of cheese
It truly was a plateful
Tom thanked them all for shredding it
Explaining he was grateful

An elephant did take a jump
And landed with great speed
On top of Mr. Collins who
Said flatly, he agreed

A teacher made a Mobius strip
The class was mystified
But despite their mass confusion
It seems that just Juan sighed

While playing poker with his friends
Tom's card count got reduced
"Someone just stole my two of hearts"
Is what this guy deduced

"I need to find a sharpener"
"This works disjointedly"
"My pencil's lead is broken bad"
Tom said disappointedly

A card came back with postage due
It made this day eventful
Now Tom will have to mail again
For that he is resentful

Tom Swiftie Verses

The lady glared at me and asked
Was I some kind of crook?
It seems her watch was missing and
She had that timeless look

At Halloween my dog dressed up
Like a cantaloupe by golly
"I have mixed feelings 'bout it though"
I said with melancholy

The plumber made the water rise
To fill my paper cup
"It's twenty feet from ground to top"
This little guy piped up

Pronunciation Matters

My friends back east
Do not catch on
They say I live
In Ory-gone

So I tell them
I am someone
Who makes his home
In Ory-gun

If we would spell it
As we say it
Arranging letters
To convey it

Then friends who live
Way out past Boise
Would get it right
Back home in Joisey

Make Merry

Make merry every single day
And you will chase the blues away
But if you choose instead to mope
There really isn't any hope

Schrödinger's Poem

Schrödinger's cat is where it's at
The unknown to discover
Alive and dead, they're both a fact
Until we lift the cover

It's not just cats that act this way
This poem's like that, believe it
Cuz it was quite a classic
Up until you chose to read it

Words of Wisdom

A quarterback got very mad
And oft would loudly mention
That his receivers very bad
Got most of the attention

His coach pulled him aside one day
And said to him, "My friend"
"The only words that I can say"
"Is all good things come to an end"

Absurdity

There really is absurdity
In modern English wordity

My English teacher thinks I'm drunk
And says that I am apt to flunk

This all because I took my phone
And matched its files from my home

When it was done the wording stunk
Instead of synched, I said it sunk

And now my grade is too

Dorothy's dog's shadow made
a Toto eclipse of the sun

The Odd Farmer's Almanac for 2021

Stare at the Watch

Asleep is awake
False is true
Endangered is safe
Old is new

Naked is clothed
Wealthy is poor
Loved is loathed
Less is more

Guilty is innocent
Pollution is green
Music is dissonant
Life is obscene

Harming is helping
Shapeless is form
Freezing is melting
Racists are norm

Winning is losing
Cheating is fair
Simple's confusing
Abandonment's care

Hotness is cold
Blackness is white
Timid is bold
Wrong's the new right

Friends are enemies
Enemies are friends
Dollars are pennies
The beginning's the end

Goodbye, My Friend

Today my friend
Went far away
'Twas great to see him
Yesterday

We had some laughs
We had some fun
But now it all
Is done

I'm very sad
To have this loss
But very happy
That our paths crossed

RIP Keith

Surviving
Tiny seedling pushing through
The soil that's all around you
Capture rays
On sunny days
Or showers just might drown you

Good Health

We want to live forever but
We're limited, you see
There is a stop watch wired into
Each one's biology

When tick, tick, ticking's getting weak
Some wish that they could find it
I suppose that if they did then they
Would grab it and rewind it

You know that's not the way it works
So, easy on the sweets
And exercise and monitor
The things each day you eat

But that just buys more time, you know
Nobody can deny it
Good health is just the slowest rate
That you can hope to die at

The Odd Farmer's Almanac for 2021

Professionals

It really hit me
Very hard
To learn bad lawyers
Get **disbarred**

And I confess
That I was shocked
Hearing bad clergymen
Get **defrocked**

So if an electrician
Gets indicted
Does it mean he will
Be **delighted**?

And if your dry cleaner's
Work's a mess
Is it likely they will
Be **depressed**?

If vintners leave you
Empty handed
Will the result be that they
Get **decanted**?

If plagiarism
Should be disclosed
Will a musician then
Be **decomposed**?

If a mathematician
Loses trust
Will the outcome be that
She's **non-plussed**?

If a builder structures
Beds of junk
Will the woodworker's union
Say he's **debunked**?

Professionals

And all those lasses
Getting kissed
Come wedding day
Are they **dismissed**?

If a bartender doesn't
Work too hard
And then gets fired,
Is she **disbarred**?

If a power plant
Gets lowly rated
Are workers there
Degenerated?

If fireplace makers
Work is mis-handled
Does that mean they will
Get **dismantled**?

If a urine test
Says a plumber's drugged
Will the union then leave
Him **unplugged**?

If a cowboy's work
Is very strange
Is the outcome he will
Be **deranged**?

And arborists who miss the mark
Or noisy guard dogs in the dark
Would you say they should
Be **debarked**?

If senators
Don't work September
Should Congress say they've
Been **dismembered**? (YES)

Senior citizens old on for dear life

Long hikes are really wanderful

The optometry school's football team is the Fighting Iris

The Odd Farmer's Almanac for 2021

Professionals

Will stenographers
Who mis-transcribed
Discover they have
Been **de-scribed**?

Can a software writer
Who is reviled
Discover she's been
Decompiled?

When magicians' tricks have
Bad conclusions
Will their union leave them
Disillusioned?

And if two nudists
Went and feuded
Do you think they should
Be **denuded**?

If a barista's drinks
Are mostly hated
Will Starbucks make them
Decaffeinated?

If what she says
Is mis-pronounced
Will an MC immediately
Be **denounced**?

If a Notary Public
Is cast aside
Or a crazy person
Becomes untied
Should they both be
Decertified?

Will an ethics professor
Who is despised
Be very quickly
Demoralized?

Professionals

If a poison maker's
Poison rocks
Do you think they should
Be **detoxed**?

Voices

Mother Nature's lovely voice
Appeals at all our ages
Hearing it can cause rejoice
No matter what our stage is

Though awkwardness of youth I had
And no one disagreed
Mother Nature pushed this lad
To go and spread his seed

I'm older now and happy too
That awkward phase long passed
Perspective I have gained, it's true
And knowledge I've amassed

When Mother Nature's in my head
Today it is regardin'
Some seed she's asking me to spread
But only for my garden

And this I do, I love it so
It's great to sprout those seedlings
There is one problem you should know
It hurts more than my feelings

My back right now is killing me
My hip has got some pain
The hoeing that I did, you see
Sure caused a lot of strain

Yes Mother Nature's song to me
Is sweet, like summer wine
But gets drowned out quite easily
By the voice of Father Time

The Odd Farmer's Almanac for 2021

DECEMBER, 2021

You might think this is not the month to be a Scrooge, but perhaps it is. If you're a Scrooge in January, saying "Bah! Humbug" is kind of silly, unless, of course, you're tired of the New Year or the Martin Luther King holiday. In either of those fits you, you've got a problem (and you're a grouch). No, if you're going to be a Scrooge, December is the PERFECT month for it because by the time the month rolls around, most people know EXACTLY where Scrooge was coming from and, if they could, they'd invite him to dinner. They're tired of Thanksgiving leftovers, coming up with gift ideas, office holiday parties, wrapping paper, and songs that go "pah rum pum pum pum."

Now maybe that's bit negative. Christmas also has mistletoe, sleigh rides, people happily singing "Let it Snow," flying reindeer, and a jolly old guy who lives at the north pole and leaves once a year to deliver toys to children all over the world. The only problem is that those are all fantasies, you know. Think hard - when was the last time you roasted a chestnut on an open fire?

While Christmas may be a fantasy, the bills that accompany it are very real. So, wait - let's see - fantasy, big bills. . . . Gadzooks! Christmas is an annual trip to Disneyland, except it involves cutting trees, hanging tinsel, and is harder to avoid.

OK, OK. I keep trying to find something nice to say about the season and I'm struggling. There are at least two other omnipresent fixtures of December (that's what I want in my stocking this year - omnipresents). The first nice things are the after Christmas sales because (of course!) there weren't enough before-Christmas sales to sell everything the stores stocked up on, so they now must unload everything they have in order to make room for the giant January sales right around the corner (of course again!).

Second is the sneakiest holiday of the year - New Year's Day, which technically occurs in January (very sneaky), but it's close enough for a writer struggling to find something good to say about December. New Year's Day really should be upsetting - it's a reminder that we're getting older. It occurs during one of the darkest times of the year. It carries with it the "luggage" of the evening before it. It is the first day of those pesky resolutions we are ABSOLUTELY going to keep this time. And yet, in spite of all those reasons not to like it, the entire world revels in its arrival the night before every single year. If Christmas had the PR agent that New Year's Day has, no one would think of Scrooge. Ah, well, a holiday can dream, can't it?

Speaking of dreamy, the December sky is just that. First off, there are NINE meteor showers - too many to name, but they occur on December 2, 6, 7, 9, 12, 14, 16, 19, and 22. The moon makes its usual close approaches to Mars (2nd), Venus (6th), Saturn (7th), Jupiter (8th), and Mars again on the 31st. If you have a fantastic telescope, you can see Pluto appear close to Venus (12th) and Mercury (28th). The moon's phases this month are new (3rd), half (10th), full (18th), and half (26th). The winter solstice (shortest day of the year and first day of winter) slides under the radar (Thank You, Christmas!) on the 21st and if that isn't enough going on in the sky for you, there is a full solar eclipse on the 4th visible in the southern hemisphere from South Africa to South America. Happy 2022 to everyone.

The Odd Farmer's Almanac for 2021

December First
1878
No word on how long
Til the first person called
The very first White House
Phone was installed

> When zen masters give up, they throw in the Tao

December Second
1964
Though it is not clear
If his singing improved
Ringo Starr very famously
Had his tonsils removed

December Third
1931
Plop, plot
Fizz, fizz
Today Alka-Seltzer
Opens for biz

December Fourth
1952
London is covered
By a very dense fog
A newly coined word
Describes it - "smog"

December Fifth
1848
President Polk relays
What he's been told
The discovery of
California gold

> The Stoned Age began with the discovery of fire and weed

December Sixth
1964
Airing for the holidays
The very first time this year
Is the TV special
"Rudolph the Red-nosed Reindeer"

> Eating uranium will give you atomic ache

December Seventh
1963
Army-Navy fans
Watching play by play
Were the very first viewers
Of instant replay

December Eighth
1931
Getting signals to television
This patent enabled
Invented today
The coaxial cable

December Ninth
1965
Good grief, it took
Long enough to be
But Charlie Brown finally
Made it to TV

December Tenth
1799
Adopting the metric system
When given the chance
The first in the world
Was the country of France

December Eleventh
1844
The giggling was very
Difficult to hide
When the first dentist used
Nitrous oxide

The first Christmas mass came from a weigh in a manger

Sunrise in London produces English lit

Charmin is hind sanitizer

The Odd Farmer's Almanac for 2021

> I failed my italic writing exam by making straight A's

December Twelfth
1792
A excellent student
From the very first session
Ludwig von Beethoven
Had his first music lesson

December Thirteenth
1774
Very loudly shouting
With a message numbing
Paul Review announces
"The British are coming"

December Fourteenth
1969
Ed Sullivan had them
Everyone should know
The Jackson Five's
First TV show

December Fifteenth
1854
For keeping their streets
Fit to be seen
Philadelphia got the first
Street cleaning machine

> Patent for Silly String issued 12/12/72

> With avian disease, it's the early worm that gets the bird

> What to give someone who has everything - Omnipresents

December Sixteenth
1950
Not all that strange
For a child star to do
Shirley Temple retires
At age twenty two

December Seventeenth
2018
The poacher's sentence
Was abundantly clear
Watching "Bambi" in prison
Repeatedly for a year

December Eighteenth
1898
An automobile
With incredible power
Set a new land speed record
39 miles per hour

December Nineteenth
1732
Benjamin Franklin
With his great knack
Began publishing
Poor Richard's Almanack

December Twentieth
1928
Off to Quebec
Starting in Maine
Dogsled mail
Bypasses the train

> Squeezing juice from a battery means pressing charges

> Bingo players have seen it all B4

December Twenty First
1891
James Naismith
Standing tall
Organizes the first
Game of basketball

December Twenty Second
1958
Alvin and Friends
Lots of fun
"The Chipmunk Song"
Hits number one

Page 106

The Odd Farmer's Almanac for 2021

Lumberjacks have 2 chopping days left til Christmas

December Twenty Third
1888
Van Gogh and Gauguin
Have an argument severe
One spites his face
By cutting off an ear

December Twenty Fourth
1818
Simple song
Simple rhyme
"Silent Night"
Sung the first time

December Twenty Fifth
337
After many years
Of being adrift
The first Christmas celebrated
On December 25th

December Twenty Sixth
1865
For some people
No invention was greater
James Mason patented
The coffee percolator

Rocky was a role with the punches

The last letter of Noel - Ironic?

Christmas trees believe in lights after death

December Twenty Seventh
1947
An important date
Everyone should know
The first airing of
"The Howdy Doody Show"

December Twenty Eighth
1612
Galileo sees Neptune
But never uncovered
That it was a planet
And had not been discovered

December Twenty Ninth
1862
Bowling sadly
Could not be prevented
After the ball for it
Got invented

December Thirtieth
1879
Thrills, chills
Song and romance
Gilbert and Sullivan's
"Pirates of Penzance"

December Thirty First
1911
On Marie Curie
Are lots of eyes
As she snags her second
Nobel Prize

"The Far Side" debuts 12/31/1979

Canada isn't real. It's only mapleleaf

"I always wanted to be somebody, but now I realize I should have been more specific."
– Lily Tomlin

"Here's something to think about: How come you never see a headline like 'Psychic Wins Lottery'?"
– Jay Leno

A Christmas Tree to Remember

I haven't set up a Christmas tree in many years, but one of the last ones I had I'll never forget, thanks to my unusual mother. To appreciate this story, you need to know a bit about her. Mom is not your standard issue mother, very unconventional in many ways. I have my oddities and non-conformities, which I acknowledge and embrace and you only need to look at her to see where I get some of my traits. She had, and still has boundless energy and a love for life and laughter. She is a most unusual person and I wouldn't have her any other way.

The Christmas tree adventure I had with her took place in 1977 when she was in her 40s and I was in my 20s. She had just entered into her new career, fresh out of school as a veterinarian and was practicing under another veterinarian at the time. I was a technician in a lab in town and neither of us really had any money to spare. The town was Stillwater, Oklahoma and she had a lot of contact with local ranchers there from her work. As Christmas season rolled around, she told me of a rancher who said she could cut down some pines on his land out of town to use as Christmas trees.

We decided to take advantage of his generosity one frosty Oklahoma evening in early December. Oklahoma is a barren place where the wind really does "come sweeping down the plain" and this was a typical night for that time of year - not exactly a Clydesdale and sleigh experience. Our sleigh and horse was a friend's ancient, rusty pickup truck lacking shock absorbers that Mom had borrowed to haul the trees.

I say trees because when she picked me up, she noted that she had promised four other people she would get them trees too, so we were in search not of one tree each for the two of us, but six. The enormity of that task didn't weigh on us as we took off "down Santa Claus way," bouncing in that rattle trap truck as it hit the numerous potholes of the red-dirt Oklahoma road leading to the tree property. Mom, as usual, drove too fast and that only added to the gyrations and squeaks of the truck.

We got to our destination, a scrap of land in the middle of nowhere, as the sun was setting and she parked the truck by the side of the road. We carried a Coleman lantern and a saw. After a hike of what seemed like two miles, thanks to getting lost in the deepening darkness, we reached a cluster of pine trees and, with Mom holding the lantern, I began my sawing. Though the cutting was strenuous, we had a great time reminiscing about Christmases past.

Finally, the cutting was done and we began the process of dragging what suddenly seemed like monster, old growth trees back to the truck, retracing our circuitous route. The lantern now was a necessity be cause the sun had long ago set and it was pitch dark and getting cold.

As we neared the road and our truck, a curious thing happened. It seemed innocent at first. A pickup truck was coming down the road where our truck was parked. It too bounced, raising dust as it careened across the same potholes we had traversed earlier. My mother, who was leading the way back with the lantern spotted the pickup, turned white as a ghost, and proceeded to jump into a drainage ditch. Then, about as much as one can exclaim in a whisper, she frantically gestured and said, "Get down!" three times, each with increasing vigor as she extinguished the lantern.

The Odd Farmer's Almanac for 2021

A Christmas Tree to Remember

Fearing God knows what was happening - moonshiners, KKKers, or a bunch of rowdies looking for trouble - I let go of the trees, dropped to the ground, and laid face down about as flat as I ever have been. The truck stopped at our truck for a minute, apparently checking it out, and then drove on. After what seemed like a longer time than I'm sure it was, I crawled, belly down like a GI in a war zone, ahead to where my mother was.

Me: "What in the hell was that about?"
Mom: "Shh"
Me: "What do you mean 'shh?' They're gone."
Mom: "They might come back"
Me: "Who are THEY?"
Mom:
Me: "Who are THEY?"
Mom: "Let's just wait here for a minute"
Me: "Why are we hiding here?"

And then it hit me.

Me: "Do you have permission to cut these trees down?"
Mom:
Me: "MOTHER! Did you get permission to cut these trees down?"
Mom:
Me: "Did you tell the owner you were going to cut down trees?"
Mom: "Sort of. Let's get these trees loaded up."

And then, partly to avoid answering my questions and partly to get away from a possible crime scene as quickly as possible, Mom started tossing trees over the fence into the road with an adrenalin-fueled vengeance that lumberjacks would have envied. We couldn't re-light the lantern because (of course!) she had run out of matches, but something as simple as darkness wasn't about to stop my mother at this point. She told me, no, she ORDERED me to get the trees loaded ASAP in the back of the truck. And with this, I came to grips with the circumstances - I was now a Christmas tree poacher, dragged into a life of crime by my mother. A life on the lam flashed before my eyes. Our Budweiser commercial had turned into Bonnie and Clyde and that particular criminal endeavor didn't have a happy ending.

Then, for the first and only time in my life, the emotions of fear and funny collided inside of me. Let me tell you, they are not designed to be experienced together. To the outside observer, it probably appeared much more comical than it felt. I simultaneously laughed and screamed at her into the darkness of the air about what we were doing, as I trembled with the cold and the fear we were going to get caught by some Christmas tree lunatic.

You know those horrible Halloween movies where a crazy killer is chasing people? The person I envisioned was scarier than any of them - the ghost of Christmas presents, as it were. Meanwhile, Mom, ever focused on the true meaning of

A Christmas Tree to Remember

Christmas as can only be experienced by smuggling Christmas trees, kept shushing me and jostling the trees in back of the truck to get them to fit. All of this only accentuated my already heightened funny and fear emotions, inducing a sort of hysteria. I collapsed behind the truck paralyzed, shaking, laughing, and terrified we were about to get caught and hauled to the sheriff.

As I was experiencing the terror and humor of all this, Mom, the Cool Hand Luke of our Laurel and Hardy operation, did a quick tie down using the tiny piece of rope she brought, grabbed me by the collar and literally drug and deposited me into the passenger side of the truck. She then dashed to the driver's side, started the truck, and, with squeal of tires, we raced homeward with six "hot" Christmas trees, traveling (lights off, of course!) at about twice our original speed over a road that was definitely NOT designed for her driving. How the trees kept from falling out, I'll never know.

Later, after the chaos was all over, Mom *claimed* she had mentioned to the owner that she *might* come by sometime and cut down one tree (not six!), but he hadn't responded. As she pointed out, he didn't say no, so she took it as a yes (of course!). It didn't matter. I had escaped the closest brush I ever had with the law, and a Merry Christmas was had by all, except possibly the rancher missing six trees. I wonder if the other four tree recipients ever learned the truth of how their trees got to them that year.

E-Tale
A certain salmon that I know
Screwed up at Christmas time
Instead of going shopping
Did all his work online
(and now he's hooked)

Present Accounted For
ESP's not news to me
I think you get my drift
I know my Christmas present
It's true - I have a gift

Xmas Wedding
Aretha Franklin, Buddy Holly
Christmas marriage, oh my golly
Festive joy - Aretha Holly

Cold Front
Frosty Snowman's favorite song
Leaves him all feeling mellow
So little children, sing along
"Freeze a Jolly Good Fellow"

Selfies put you in your own youniverse

Picket Lyin'
With Santa's helpers now on strike
He cannot help himself
I'm thinking that this Christmas time
Will be the first Noelf

Haute Tub
Global warming is for real
Don't think that I'm a fool
The evidence is Santa
Now lives at the North Pool

On the Roof
Santa Claus has got it made
Though some of us may grouse
He never pays for parking cuz
It's always on the house

No, Virginia
In Santa that kid will not believe
I do not know the cause
I guess it's safe to say that he's
A rebel without a Claus

The Odd Farmer's Almanac for 2021

Miscellaneous Christmas Verses

Crabs below the ocean
Like Christmas time because
It's when they all get visited
By good old Sandy Claws

For my wife, I sought a toaster
I should have planned ahead
I couldn't buy the ten slice one
I was running low on bread

The snowman's kid at Christmas time
Is in "timeout" I found
Apparently it seems that he
Was having a meltdown

An ornament's in treatment now
For addictive-type disease
It seems that he's been fighting it
Since he got hooked on Christmas trees

Computer gamers in Bethlehem
Could make our Christmas stranger
Instead of a kid and three wise men
They'd put a Wii in a manger

St. Nick to me is wonderful
All loving, kind, and gentle
My emotions overflow for him
Cuz I am Santamental

There's so much more to Santa Claus
Than Dasher, Donner, Prancer
In fact, I hear he has some very
Talented pole dancers

A very wise person said to me
That crime really never pays
Consider the Advent calendar thief
Who just got 25 days

The brightly twinkling Christmas light
Says his savings all are gone
Because this holiday season
He's working off and on

A shooting at the North Pole
I'd advise that you stay tuned
Early reports suggest it was
An elf-inflicted wound

And speaking of elves, old Santa Claus
Used them since he began
He easily could be described
As a real elf made man

I eat too much at Christmas time
And it treats me most foul-ly
That's why they sing this time of year
"Tis the season to be jowly"

Santa likes his picture took
It gives him quite a kick
And now he does it by himself
With his new elfie stick

One of Santa's reindeer
Drinks too much and it shows
The others call him Brewdolph
And he has a big red nose

Santa ate the cookies I left for him
Though he left behind a fume
I never thought I'd have to go
And Santatize our bathroom

A Christmas tree believes, you see
With its last Earthly breath
That there is more to follow
You know, lights after death

Ken dolls from Santa's helpers are elf-made men

The Odd Farmer's Almanac for 2021

Miscellaneous Christmas Verses

The snowman family has problems and
They're worrying out loud
Because it seems on Christmas eve
That Frosty's gotten plowed

When the unwrapping is done
I'm sure you can guess
It is the time to celebrate
The true meaning of Christmess

One thing that Frosty will not drink
Is hot chocolate on a whim
The problem as he states it is
It goes right straight through him

Santa cannot find his wife
Since she reached menopause
He strikes it to experience
Knowing she is a lost Claus

On Christmas eve, I tied one on
I guess it was a case
Of really sleeping like a log because
I woke up in the fireplace

The first Noel
Way back when
Took place, of course
In Bethehem

The winter cold of Christmas eve
Is just how we prefer
To recall all of the memories
Of the way we brrrrrrrrr

It's Christmas season
That's the reason
Everyone is merry
I'll pick for me
A random tree
Something arbortrary

I loved what I got Christmas day
A wonderful clock came my way
I just had to shriek
It was so unique
There's no present like the time, I say

An Oregon Christmas

It's wintertime in Oregon
The clouds have all come back
Most leaves are gone, the moss is out
And all the ducks go "quack!"

Our pumps are sumping merrily
In the dark and dingy cold
And lovers don't use mistletoe
They just stand under mold

A true sign of the season really
Raises my eyebrows
Whene'er I sight the first of winter's
Squadron of rain plows

Dear Santa if you come our way
And think you fly with eagles
Beware the air you breathe out here
Cuz marijuana's legal

Alas the spring's three months away
And summer's three months more
My wife's attacking mildew and
It looks like it is war

I end this verse with festive thoughts
Amidst a wintry view
Happy Holidays to everyone
The millennium's twenty two

Jelly filling is a good roll middle

Happy 2022

'Twas the night before New Year
Here in my hometown
There was moss in the trees
And rain coming down

The presents had all been
Unwrapped with great glee
But with Christmas now over
Time to take down the tree

Ma's drinking pinot
And I've got a beer
We're sitting and pondering
The upcoming year

We're both much in favor
Of hope, love and peace
But please, most of all
No more COVID disease

Egg Noggin'

Last night was very loud
I hope today is quiet-y
Because my head is hurting,
ow!
The result of auld langxiety

New Year's Grieve
On every New Year
I lament
The weight I've gained
By snaccident

Do pennies from heaven mean change is in the air?

Respect the Farmers

A farmer works all day a seedin'
Sprouting tiny cotyledons
Toil in heat and rain and snow
Results in many things that grow

And with each teeny weenie flower
Growers harvest solar power
So think before you go insult your
People doing agriculture

No Hard Fillings

A patient
To the dentist went
Because he lost his filling

The dentist gent
Then underwent
A bunch of noisy drilling

When he got done
The dental one
Said something very chilling

"Beware, the pain"
"May come again"
"When you receive my billing"

Pizza Cake

They put some pizza in your hands
You love it, order more
Your hunger for this stuff expands
They bring it to your door
Your craving for their product grows
Much stronger than for sex
At this point you are in the throes
Of the Dominoes' effects

The Odd Farmer's Almanac for 2021

Shorties

Not for Checkout
The librarian's left me
All unhooked
When I asked for a date
She said she's booked

The Price Ain't Right
To the auction I went
With keen intent
But ended up with
Bidder disappointment

"Let Meowt"
I just heard a pun
That's truly the worst
It said cat poetry
Is really purrverse

Seeing the Future
There was a singer
I recently saw
Who sang 'Do-Re-Mi'
I knew he'd go 'Fa'

Dis Stilled
And back in France
It's really odd
Their holy water
Is "Eau, my god"

Instru Mental
I'm guessing I must
Have broken a rule
By pulling those strings
To pass harp school

Random Tweet
Birds are better
Off I guess
Pursuing life, liberty
And happy nests

Mow and Mow
The local landscaper
Is my buddy Jim
He's a good friend because
I get a lawn with him

The Illiterati
For a girl that I loved
I should have persisted
She had only four vowels
Didn't know I existed

Tasty
Go tell your tale
It's worth defending
Your pretzel making story
Has a happy bending

Movie Buzz
That honey making video
Is really groovy
I recommend highly
A good bee movie

Jolly Roger
I guess I know whom
To focus ire at
That guy stole my lunch
The chicken pot pirate

Nearest Neighbor
I don't know the hows,
Or whys or whethers
But why are "apart"ments
Close together?

Dibs
The chicken? The egg?
Who was first? No matta
We'll never know
From poultry data

Rush Hour
The rush for postage
Is indeed
A really truly
Big stampede

Down Under
Those Aussies have
Unusual ways
When they're celebrating
Their Perth days

Aroma Wasn't Built . . .
The expensive perfume
She wears to events
Suggests that lady
Has no common scents

Stroke of Bad Luck
A painter got in trouble
The cop said he saw
"This individual had"
"A bad brush with the law"

Shut Up
The door closing contest
In Amsterdam
Concludes today
With the grand slam

Comeback
I'm proud of a retort
I made in the spring
Some said it was
Quite a May zing'

Snooze Blues
Please be quiet
Do not shout
I'm in the top bunkbed
Over and out

Wetted Down
Water addiction?
Most unusual
Drinking too much
May leaves you dilutional

On Tap
When retirement comes
No need to beg
I invest in beer
With my 401 keg

Low and Inside
The baseball fan
Expressed dislike
When the umpire's union
Declared a strike

The Odd Farmer's Almanac for 2021

Dream of Consciousness

Is life a dream of consciousness
From beings way up high?
Who go to sleep when we're awake
Then rise when bedtime's nigh?

If so, we're mere illusions
Of brains that aren't our own
And what we call existence
Comes from their thoughts alone

That makes us puppets, everyone
We dance, we sing, we love
Because of neural firing
In super brains above

What can we do? Can we escape?
And then spring into being?
Or are we mental prisoners
Of what those brains are dreaming?

I do not know the answer, but
I am most disinclined
To be a dream of consciousness
In someone else's mind

My Buddy Stan

My buddy Stan
Is living life
He's had his kids
He loves his wife

He's had his moments
Setbacks too
Fought for what
Is right and true

And never did
The man complain
When docs took pieces
Of his brain

We go way back
To Illinois
Where both of us
Were little boys

Twas so much fun
When we would play
Made Michael
Disappear one day

Whene'er it snowed
We'd ride our sleds
And go toss walnuts
At Goldie's shed

I'm thinking how
He's loving life
And dealing with
The mental strife

He is a brave one
Quite the man
This ode's for you
My buddy Stan

Wanted: Dead or Alive - Schrodinger's Cat

All We Need is Love

The road that makes a country great
Cannot be paved with words of hate

If it is true our course is shifting
The bottom's where we should be lifting

Cuz no one can be left behind
If prosperity we hope to find

Let's look out for each other, friends
Love's the way this nonsense ends

I got my start writing verses by writing song lyric parodies, a la Weird Al. A lot of the stuff I write is about the subject I am trained in - biochemistry. I write on other topics too, though, and one of them is about my home in western Oregon. This is a song I wrote about the Oregon rain and it seems like a good way to end the almanac. If you'd like to download a free recording of it, please go to my Web site, www.davincipress.com

Let It Rain
(to the tune of "*Let It Snow*")

Oh the Oregon weather's dowdy
'Cause the sky is mostly cloudy
It won't stop if you complain
So let it rain, let it rain, let it rain

It doesn't show signs of slowing
And it's rarely right for snowing
Though it's driving some folks insane,
Let it rain, let it rain, let it rain

When it finally turns out dry
We'll be putting away our rain gear
It will probably be July
But I'll surely miss the rain dear

'Cuz the sound of the falling rain
Pitter pattering down the drain
Makes music inside my brain
So let it rain, let it rain, let it rain

The Odd Farmer's Almanac for 2021

The Reviews Are In

"Almanac of the year!!" - Time
"A daily dose of laughs!!" - NYT
"Never laughed so hard!" - Village Voice
"Laughed so hard I cried!!"
"I laughed AND cried!"
"Laughed through tears of joy!"
"I cried spaghetti!"
"You what?!!"
"I cried spaghetti"
"You can't cry spaghetti!"
"Yes, I did. Red stuff all over my collar!!"
"That was ketchup!!"
"OK. I cried ketchup!"
"You spilled ketchup from your french fries"
"I didn't have french fries!!"
"Sorry. Onion rings"
"It was because I was crying so much!!"
"It's not the same"
"Is too!!"
"Not"
"Is too!!!"
"Stop with the exclamation points, already"
"Can't!!"
"Can too"
"Can't!!"
"This isn't going anywhere"
"Let's get some onion rings!!"

Robbin' Hoods

A thief was robbing fabric stores
Investigators learned
They caught him rather easily
Because his work had patterns

But once he was in custody
A big surprise resulted
When officers all looked away
The criminal simply bolted

(Thanks to Indira Rajagopal
for the idea)

**Canada isn't real.
It's only mapleleaf**

The Vacuum Cleaner

And now I have
A final thought
I share it here with you

When cleaning out
A vacuum cleaner
You're a vacuum cleaner too

Page 117

About the Author

The *"Odd Farmer's Almanac for 2021"* was written by Kevin Ahern, a Professor Emeritus of Biochemistry & Biophysics at Oregon State University. Kevin has been writing limericks, verses, and similar things every day since 2012. He has numerous books out. A partial list is below. Links to places to buy all of his books are available at his Web site - www.davincipress.com

Some of Kevin's Other Books

A Limerick a Day for a Year
A Limerick a Day for Another Year
A Limerick a Day for a Third Year
A Limerick a Day for a Fourth Year
A Limerick a Day for a Fifth Year
A Limerick a Day for a Sixth Year
Limericks Come Alive!
A Turn for the Verse
Good for the Mirth
Rhymes and Misdemeanors
My Many Merry Melodies
Biochemistry Free and Easy (textbook - free)
Biochemistry Free For All (textbook - free)
Kevin and Indira's Guide to Getting Into Medical School (free)

Manufactured by Amazon.ca
Bolton, ON